Live to Write Another Day

A Survival Guide for Screenwriters and Creative Storytellers

By Dean Orion

Published in the United States by Sky Father Media
ISBN 978-0-9890593-1-2

Acknowledgements

The writing of this book would not have been possible without the love and support of my beautiful wife, Rochelle, and incredible daughters, Eden and Avalon. I want to especially thank my pal Sybil Grieb, for inspiring me to take a leap of faith and go on this wild ride, and Christian Knudsen, who has not only been an incalculable resource, but a truly supportive friend. The boundless talent of Mark Page, who created the cover art, never ceases to amaze me. And I can't even begin to describe how much I appreciate the work of Jodi Lester, whose editorial knowledge and invaluable work on this book have been both a Godsend and an education. Lastly, I am so very grateful to my brother Marc, who is always my most trusted read, and my dear friends Tom Teicholz, Maria Alexander, Trey Callaway, and Karey Kirkpatrick, who were also generous enough to read early drafts and provide blurbs for The Writer Gene website.

1. The Writer Gene

I was eleven years old when I wrote my first original story. It was the story of triplets separated at birth. One becomes a professional football player, one a rodeo champ, and the other a successful Hollywood actor. Then, lo and behold, at the ripe old age of twenty-one, they learn that they're long lost brothers!

This could only have meant one thing. Either I had a serious personality disorder, or I was born to be a writer. Frankly, I think the jury's still out.

I rarely go back and reread anything I've written over the years, especially the early stuff, but not too long ago when I was in the throes of moving, I stumbled upon my original copy of "Triplets" and couldn't quite resist the temptation (not to mention the fact that it was a wonderful respite from the drudgery of packing boxes). Naturally, I got to thinking about how far I've come as a writer, how much I've learned, and how much I'd like to share with other writers, which is how the idea for this survival guide was born.

Needless to say, I was quite amused with myself as I read through that ancient manuscript. Like most kids, I had a pretty active imagination, which was obvious from the very first paragraph.

There was no doubt I was having a lot of fun when I wrote it, absolutely relishing that magical moment in my life when I suddenly came to understand the power of words and how to manipulate them. But the thing that truly astonished me about this younger version of myself was the innate ability that I possessed, even at that tender age, to construct what was clearly a very sophisticated story. No one had taught me about the nuances of creative writing or storytelling, and to my recollection, Mrs. Shertzer's sixth-grade class at Fifth Avenue Elementary School wasn't exactly a hotbed of budding literary geniuses. Yet somehow, intuitively, I was able to create this perfect three-act structure for my "Triplets" masterpiece, a well-defined beginning, middle, and end that wove seamlessly back and forth between my three protagonists, built to an exciting climax, and paid off quite beautifully when it was all said and done.

Now don't get me wrong, I'm not telling you this heart-warming little tale to toot my own horn. Okay, maybe I am a little bit, but that's beside the point. All I'm trying to say is that writing is in my DNA. It's not just what I do, it's who I am. In other words, for better or worse, I was born with the *writer gene*.

So what does this mean? What's the prognosis for someone with this dreaded affliction, doc? Well, if you too are the proud owner of this lovely piece of biochemistry, then you know exactly what it means. It means that as much as you struggle to overcome your shortcomings or to be recognized for your achievements as a writer, as much as you get rejected, as much as you try to do other things with your life or make a living in other ways— even if you *have* to make a living in other ways— there's just no chance in hell that you'll ever stop writing. It's like trying to defy gravity. It's physically impossible.

In my experience, I've found that members of our little gene pool generally respond to this stark reality in one of two ways: either they do what I do most of the time, which is to be honest and admit how much they *love* writing, despite how incredibly hard it is to do well; or they do what I only do every now and again, which is to endlessly bitch, moan, and complain about how much they *hate* writing, because of how incredibly hard it is to do well. By the way, it's also not at all unusual to hear a writer do both of these things simultaneously, sometimes in the very same long and laborious sentence, like I just did.

All joking aside though, the truth is I really do love writing. I love it because it helps me make sense of a world that very often makes no sense at all; because it gives me a structure in which to express myself, to create order out of chaos, to be the master of the universe, even if it is a make-believe universe. Most importantly, I love writing because I love the creative process, the journey that you go on when you conceive of an idea and, like Odysseus, feel compelled to find the path through every obstacle, every trial and tribulation, in an effort to realize that idea's full potential and bring it safely home.

If you're like me and you have the writer gene, then I'm sure you're in the midst of your own writing odyssey. And, like me, you could probably use a little help every now and then, a little reassurance that you're not alone out there, blowing aimlessly in the middle of the Mediterranean. That's what this survival guide is all about. It's my way of helping you—my writer brethren—navigate those often unpredictable, sometimes murky waters, in any small way I can.

I've been a professional writer since the time I graduated from college, which is about twenty-five years now. In that time I've written advertising copy, stage plays, screenplays, teleplays, website content, and all different kinds of interactive games and theme-park experiences. It's been an eclectic career to be sure, but each of these creative challenges has, in its own unique way, taught me very valuable lessons and invariably contributed to my overall growth, both as a person and as an artist. I don't profess to know everything or have the end-all-be-all, sure-fire secret to being a great writer. Let's be real, no one does. What I *do* know is there are aspects of my creative process and my psychological approach to the craft of writing that are very effective and could potentially work for you as well.

So whether you're a high school kid with big dreams, a person who's spent half your life in another career neglecting your writer gene, or even a seasoned vet who just needs a little pep talk, it's my sincerest hope that there's a word or two in this little tome that will help you weather every storm, sail past every siren, and slay every monster as you tell that great story that simply must be told.

SURVIVAL GUIDE SUMMARY

1. The Writer Gene

Things to Remember:

- If you're a person who is driven to tell stories with words, then you have the writer gene.

- Guess what—you're not alone.

2. The Art of Procrastination

I think it's only fitting to begin a discussion of the creative process with a little procrastination. As you might have already guessed from the title of this chapter, I think procrastination gets a bad rap. Why? Because I wholeheartedly believe that procrastination is *part* of the creative process. There. I said it. You happy? I hope so, because I'm not just trying to be cute. I mean it.

Now that I've gotten that off my chest, we should probably give procrastination a more positive name, don't you think? How about *Pre-writing*? *Braincharging*? *Mindframing*? Sound better? I think so. But let's not kid ourselves either. Regardless of what you call it, it still basically boils down to the same thing—delaying the inevitable reality that at some point you have to get on with it, just dive into the deep end of the pool and start paddling. Which is bad, right? Delaying. Avoiding. Not doing what you're supposed to be doing. Worst of all, wasting time. Right?

You see what I'm doing here? I can't psychologically reconcile the fact that for every minute of my life I'm not writing, I feel terribly guilty, like I'm not getting a damn thing done. "Come on people, we're burning daylight!" the drill sergeant in my head says. "But I can't just start typing," I plead. "I'm not ready!"

My point here is this:

Procrastinating is only bad if you create anxiety around the fact that you're procrastinating.

Okay, let's say you can get past the guilt. You no longer feel bad about the time you're spending rearranging the furniture or trying to peel the perfect cucumber. How the hell is that part of the process? The answer is that creative writing requires a very unique type of focus where you are at once a passive and active channel of information. You are both passively *listening* to the ideas coming into your head at a million miles per second and actively *talking* as you compose the words. But believe it or not, when you're procrastinating you're actually starting to engage in this process, because you're already thinking about the story that you're telling, even if it's only subconsciously.

Procrastination comes in as many varieties as there are writers. Some people watch YouTube videos. Some people clean the house. Some people go for a walk. Me, I'm a football junkie, so I like to read all the latest and greatest happenings of the National Football League before I put pen to paper (even in the off-season). Any and all forms are acceptable as far as I'm concerned. Procrastination is an equal opportunity employer.

Not that *chronic procrastination*, to the point where you don't ever actually write anything, is okay. That's obviously not what I'm talking about. There's a point at which that kind of thing begins to call into question whether you actually possess the writer gene in the first place. What I am saying is that procrastinating is pretty much the universal starting point of the writing process, a way of getting yourself into the *alpha state*, as the scientists would say. So whatever it is that you have to do to get yourself there, don't beat yourself up about it. Just accept it, embrace it, and know that your fellow writers all over the world, from amateurs to Pulitzer Prize winners, are at the very same moment doing exactly the same thing.

SURVIVAL GUIDE SUMMARY

2. The Art of Procrastination

Things to Remember:

- Procrastination is part of the creative process.

- Procrastination is only bad if you create anxiety about procrastinating. Don't beat yourself up about it. Use it.

- You are both a passive and active channel of information when you write.

Questions to Ask Yourself:

- What procrastination activities contribute to your process? Make a list.

- What procrastination activities are destructive to your process? Make a list.

- How much procrastination time will you allow yourself when you sit down to write? Be specific.

3. The Write Environment

Getting into that alpha state goes hand in hand with another very important aspect of creative writing—the environment in which you write.

Though some people have no issues whatsoever writing in a noisy environment, like a coffee shop or a restaurant, most of us need some relatively quiet space where it's a little easier to concentrate. I'm generally in the quiet camp, but there are also specific components of the process that I find I can do almost anywhere. Not surprisingly, I tend to be fine in a louder environment for the more active aspects of the job, like brainstorming, concepting, and outlining. On the other hand, I usually need a more serene environment for tasks that involve more passive listening and comprise the heavy-lifting part of the process. For instance, if I'm focused on dialogue, I tend to require a pretty cloistered-type space. Writing dialogue is probably the most passive thing you do as a writer, as you are basically listening to people talk in your head and acting like a stenographer.

Consistency

Up until the day my first child was born, I pretty much always wrote at home. My wife was around here and there, but she was usually busy with her own stuff, so the house was, for the most part, a fairly serene place. Newborn infants, however, are not always very accommodating, as anyone who's had one will attest. Consequently, when our first little girl came along, I found myself in dire need of a place where I could go to get my "alpha state on." I could have looked for office space somewhere, but I wasn't too keen on spending the money, so I continued to pursue other options and eventually arrived at a very attractive alternative.

One of my best friends is an acupuncturist. My ingenious plan was to ask him if I could use his office after hours and write at his desk when no one else was around. Fortunately, he was very amenable to this arrangement. All I had to do was promise to keep the place clean and not stick needles in anybody in his absence. I didn't know it at the time, but this actually turned out to be a very significant development in my writing life, because now I actually had a set schedule in which I *had* to write or else I knew I would never get anything done. I could come in every evening at around six p.m. and work as late as I liked. On the weekends, the place was all mine.

The significance of having a place like this is huge. One of the best screenwriters of all time, Woody Allen once said that eighty percent of success in life is just showing up. I couldn't agree more. I'd also say that it's a whole lot easier to show up when you actually have a place *to show up to.* You may not be as lucky as I am to have a friend who's willing to share his or her space, but you may have other options. *Consistency* is the key. The best gift you can give yourself as a writer is to find that special spot where you can go, day in and day out, with little or no threat of it suddenly becoming unavailable to you. This is your safe house, your asylum, where your writer gene is always free to express itself.

By the way, my eldest daughter just turned seventeen and guess where I'm sitting right now as I write this? Oh how time flies in the asylum!

Environmental Association

In addition to providing consistency, my buddy's office also provides me with other benefits (some of them quite unexpected) that have definitely made me more productive.

For one thing, there aren't any of my own distractions and temptations around (bills to pay, dogs to walk, TV to watch, etc.). Second, I always have to be mindful that I'm a guest and that everything has to be neat, tidy, and presentable when I leave. It is, after all, his place of business, and that must be respected. This simple fact keeps me focused on what I'm there to do, which is to write. But by far the biggest benefit is how I have come to associate the space itself with successful writing. To this day, I literally start to feel the rush of alpha waves come over me as I walk through the door. It's as if my body is programmed to be productive simply because of the physical location in which I have placed it— which gives me the peace of mind that whenever I come up against a tough creative challenge, I absolutely know that I can solve it when I step into that room.

Changing the Scenery

As much as I cherish working in my buddy's office, I also think it's important to have multiple environments, other *writing silos* where you can work and be stimulated by a change of scenery. As I mentioned, there are times when I will go to a coffee shop or a restaurant, but it's usually not for more than an hour or two, and it's usually only to brainstorm or do more high-concept type work. In this case, it's the *change* that provides the creative spark I'm looking for, not necessarily the location itself.

I also belong to a place called The Writers Junction, which is a shared office-type space near my home in Santa Monica, California. Membership at The Writers Junction ranges from about $80 to $140 per month, depending on the package you choose. There are a couple of private rooms, but mostly writers share a number of larger "quiet rooms" where they sit alongside one another, similar to the way you would if you went to a public library. All the members are professional, respectful of one another, and serious about their careers, which makes it a very positive atmosphere. There is also something to be said for simply being around other writers, both for the camaraderie and the common energy, rather than being alone in a room all the time. So, if there's a place like this near you, I would highly recommend checking it out.

Bottom line:

As a creative writer you can't underestimate the role the environment you write in plays in shaping your work.

SURVIVAL GUIDE SUMMARY

3. The Write Environment

Things to Remember:

- To be productive on a regular basis, find environments that are consistently available to you.

- Make sure these environments have limited distractions and temptations. All you really need is a desk, a chair, and a power outlet.

- If an environment works for you, keep using it! It won't take long for you to associate it with successful writing, which will help build your confidence.

- A change of scenery sometimes helps the creative flow.

Questions to Ask Yourself:

- Which parts of your process can you do in a noisier environment, and which require absolute quietude? Make a list.

- Of the different environments available to you, which can you work in on a consistent basis? Can you make each of them a reliable writing silo?

- What are the available hours of each of your writing silos? Make a list.

- How many hours on any given day do you need to spend in each silo to be productive? Plan it out ahead of time.

- Is there a place near you where other writers write? It's always good to be around other writers.

4. Writer's Bl%#k

Let me ask you…why do you think I've written this widely known expression as if it were a cuss word?

Because writer's bl%#k is complete bulls%#t, that's why! It's a myth, a psychological illusion, a not-so-clever phrase that evil, spiteful people who clearly *don't* have the writer gene have created in order to keep us writers down!

That rant may be a tad overly dramatic, I admit, but the part about it being a myth—that's absolutely true. There is no such thing as writer's bl%#k. Every problem in the universe (including that problem you're currently having in the middle of your story) has a solution. Your job is to find it. If you're having difficulty, it's not because you have writer's bl%#k, it's simply because you haven't yet unearthed that particular piece of the puzzle, the operative word being *yet*.

After all the years I've been writing, it amazes me how often this issue still rears its ugly head. In fact, I think there's been a point in almost every script I've ever written where I've said to myself: "Oh my God, I've invested months of my life into this thing and it's never going to work!" This is usually followed by a lot of pacing, worrying, and handwringing, during which time

I proceed to question just about every decision I've made about it. This could go on for hours, days, or even as much as a week, though thankfully in my case it's usually resolved within twenty-four to forty-eight hours.

Why does this crisis moment inevitably strike, and if this isn't writer's bl%#k, then what the hell is?

The honest answer to the first part of the question is: I have no idea. All I know is that it happens to every writer I know, regardless of their level of experience. It'll happen to me again, and it will happen to you too, so be prepared. As for the second part, I repeat:

There is no such thing as writer's bl%#k.

What *is* this crisis thing then?

To be blunt, it's just panic. It's not an inability to find the answer. It's the sudden overwhelming feeling that the answer will never come. But the truth is, it's just a temporary state, a mirage in the midst of the desert. Understanding this phenomenon is the first step in solving any creative problem. By simply knowing in your heart, without a shadow of a doubt, that the solution exists, you've already got half the battle won. From there it's just a matter of trust that with time and a little persistence your process will eventually cause the mirage to evaporate and lead you to the promised land. This means that it's incumbent upon you to develop a process that you can rely on, a process that will give you the confidence and the fortitude to stare down that fear time after time.

All right, so now that we've dispelled this silly little myth, let's get down to brass tacks and talk about that process.

SURVIVAL GUIDE SUMMARY

4. Writer's Bl%#k

Things to Remember:

- Writer's bl%#k is a myth. Every creative problem has a creative solution.

- All writers experience crisis moments.

- Knowing that the solution to the crisis exists is half the battle.

- The other half of the battle is having a process that you can rely on.

- Breathe.

Questions to Ask Yourself:

- Have you run into this problem before? Most of the time the answer is "yes." How did you solve it last time?

- If you haven't run into this specific problem before, how is it similar to other problems you've encountered?

- How long did it take you to solve your last crisis? Be conscious of this time factor. There's usually a pattern.

- What is the strongest aspect of your core concept? Are you still speaking to it or have you strayed? Don't panic. Just take some time to re-examine the big picture.

- Is there a specific place earlier in your story (preceding the crisis point) that is not quite as solid as you thought? Take a good look. This is probably the root of your problem.

- Are you remembering to breathe?

5. Tuning In the Radio

When I was in my freshman year of college, I took an introductory philosophy course where we spent an entire semester studying a single book: *The Republic* by Plato. If you're familiar with this classic work you'll recall that within Plato's complex dialogue there is an extensive discussion about the nature of reality, at the end of which he concludes that the "thought form of a thing" is more real than the material object itself. The reasoning behind this is that nothing in the material world could ever be as pure or as perfect as the way you imagine it in your mind, so therefore it could never be as complete or true. Heady stuff, I know, but bear with me here.

What is it that we're actually trying to do when we write? We're trying to bring a thought —in the case of creative or dramatic writers, a story—into material existence. But as Plato or anyone with the writer gene will tell you, that story never seems to make it onto the page quite the way it was intended.

Now remember what I said earlier about solutions to problems existing *out there* somewhere? It's the exact same thing with original stories. They exist, I believe, as thought forms, floating around the ether in an absolutely perfect state. But when you first stumble onto one, you can't quite make it out entirely. It's kind of fuzzy and unclear, like a faint radio signal. Before you know it, you get a little curious about this signal and you start to tune it in. You try to listen to it a little closer. And closer...and closer...until finally you get this feeling deep in your belly that this is not just any random radio signal. It's a very specific signal that must be paid attention to. Now you make it your business to tune it in. This is the point when the writer gene starts to express itself, and the point where my process begins.

Getting Started with Research

Over the years I've found that I'm much more likely to make a script work if I start by researching the subject I'm writing about. To non-fiction writers, this is a no-brainer. "Of course you want to spend time researching the subject first," they would say. If you're a creative writer, however, sometimes you get so jazzed about an idea, so pumped up by that initial rush of inspiration, that you just want to jump right in and start writing. Unfortunately, I have fallen into this trap more than once and it's a recipe for disaster, an almost 100% guarantee that your crisis moment will come sooner rather than later.

Why? Because you simply haven't spent enough time tuning in this story to execute it properly.

When I begin thinking about the idea that has somehow slipped into my brain and woken me up in the middle of the night, the first thing I do is surf the web. I'm not talking about anything exhaustive, just your basic Google search to see what interesting information floats to the surface. Then, after a couple days of bookmarking, downloading, and printing the various materials, I will buy about six to eight non-fiction books that more specifically support the angle from which I'm attacking the story.

Now, you might think this approach sounds good if you're writing a crime story about the Russian mafia or a medical drama about heart surgeons, but not if you're writing a romantic comedy. There's not really much to research if your story is just about people and their relationships, right?

Actually, that's not entirely true. Granted, a romantic comedy may not always rely as heavily on the underpinnings of a particular subject, and may not require quite as much research as a crime story or a medical story, but like all stories it does have characters who must come from somewhere, who must have jobs, personal histories, and/or interests that need to be fleshed out and made three dimensional. The truth is…

There is always something that you can learn from doing a little research that will help you tell your story—any type of story.

What's more, the actual content of the research is only part of what I'm after. Hang with me here. There's a method to my madness.

The Launching Pad

Once I have all the books, I begin the passive part of the process by simultaneously reading, highlighting, and taking tons of handwritten notes on a yellow legal pad. The notes are a combination of direct quotes from various texts, my interpretations of what I'm reading, and ideas about my story that are now starting to emerge. These could include ideas for scenes or characters, high-level structural ideas with respect to how I will lay the whole thing out, thoughts on the message I'm trying to convey, or anything else about the story that pops into my head.

The key here is:

I do not edit what I write on the pad or try to make any sense of it at this point.

Why is this so important? Because again, I'm not trying to impose my will on the story. I'm trying to tune it in. It already exists, remember?

But at this stage I can't quite hear the signal clearly yet, so I have to be careful not to overthink it, and to avoid being judgmental about anything I come up with. After all, they're just ideas and nobody but me is going to read them anyway, so who cares how wacky, stupid, or off the wall they are?

This probably sounds like a painstaking process. I'm not going to lie to you, it does require a lot of discipline and patience, but once you get into it, it's really kind of liberating. You just have to commit to it, completely lose yourself in it, and keep devouring all that information until you feel like you're going to burst, like you've just eaten Thanksgiving dinner and are so stuffed you can't possibly eat another bite. This is when you know the researching phase is over and it's time to let the active part of the writing process begin. (Depending on what else I have going on in my life and what other projects I'm simultaneously working on, this *yellow-pad period* is usually about a three- to six-week deal for me.)

At this point, if I've done it right, I've read all or most of the books cover to cover, and I've compiled at least two or three legal pads full of notes. Now all I have to do is simply open up a new document on my computer and transcribe them. This is the easiest part of the entire process. There's absolutely no pressure. I'm not even writing really. I'm just typing. Sure, if I have another idea or two while I'm doing this, I'll throw it in there, but I don't feel obligated to. I'm working for minimum wage right now, essentially being my own temp secretary. Then when I'm done transcribing, I just name the file with the working title of the story and the qualifier "Notes."

What does all this stream-of-consciousness, Thanksgiving dinner bloat buy you? Well, if you begin the process of writing your original story the way I've described, you will now find yourself with at least five to ten written pages (your "Notes Document"), which means you have just successfully kicked off your project without ever having to stare at a blank page.

The Concept Document

I admit, this five to ten pages is really nothing more than a bunch of brain spasms you had while reading all those books, but when you finally go back and review the notes that you've made, I guarantee you'll be surprised at how much good stuff you've actually captured.

The important thing to understand is this:

By letting yourself passively receive this information and simply be the channel through which it flows, you can effectively get out of the way of the story, which exists in its perfect and purest form entirely separate from you.

Now you are much more equipped to tune in the rest of the story, because not only have you learned a tremendous amount about the world in which it takes place, you have also identified many of the emotional anchor points that drew you to the idea in the first place. It's around these anchor points that you can now begin to build what I call a "Concept Document."

Depending on the type of story I'm telling and the medium in which I'm telling it, the contents of my Concept Document will vary. If I'm writing a television pilot, for example, I usually like to include a section on potential future episodes, and very often I'll include a paragraph or two on various long-range character arcs. If, on the other hand, I'm creating an interactive game or experience, those types of elements may not apply. But if interactivity is involved I will definitely need to include a section on the user interface (i.e., how the consumer will interact with the various parts of the experience). Regardless of the medium, however, the five basic sections I typically include in each of my Concept Documents are:

- *Logline*
- *Theme*
- *Tone*
- *Characters*
- *Story Summary*

Whether you're writing a stage play, an original television pilot, a screenplay, a novel, a narrative-based interactive game, or any other type of original story, it's critical that you are able to articulate each of these elements with as much clarity as possible *before* you start writing the script. Again, patience is a virtue. You're still early in the tuning process. Don't rush it.

The challenge of writing a good Concept Document is to be able to take all those notes you've written during your research phase and distill them into a concise vision of what your script will eventually become. To illustrate this, I've provided the relevant sections from a Concept Document for a TV pilot called *Scotty's Travels*, which I wrote "on spec" (i.e., creating a story/script *speculatively* with the hope that you will sell it once it's written). I'm proud to say this script was honored in *Written By*, the magazine of the Writers Guild of America, as one of the best unproduced television scripts of 2004 (a dubious honor, I know, but an honor nonetheless!).

Let's take this section by section:

Getting the logline right helps you boil the story down to its essence. It's the *elevator pitch*, the *TV guide blurb*. Here's how I did it for this particular concept:

> *Logline:*
> SCOTTY'S TRAVELS *chronicles the adventures of Dr. Jonathon Scott, a prominent psychiatrist whose life is turned upside down when he's suddenly visited by an imaginary voice.*

I like to try and get the logline down to one concise sentence like this, but it could be a little longer if necessary. Just think about how you would tell someone your story if you only had about fifteen or twenty seconds to do it.

Now let's look at the theme. Identifying your theme allows you to hone your message and solidify it in your mind. You can't tell a good story if you don't have a clue as to what you're trying to say with it. I generally dig a little deeper into this one, but still try to keep it relatively short and sweet:

Theme:
This voice, whom Scotty dubs "Liberty," magnifies discordant feelings already deep within him—that his career has gone awry, and that his purpose in life is still largely unfulfilled. To remedy this, Liberty encourages Scotty to make a daring choice—to give up all he has and go out and truly heal the troubled hearts and minds of the world.

But obliging Liberty comes with a heavy price. Not only is Scotty stigmatized as a crazy person, but where he must now go, his wife and children cannot follow.

At the heart of Scotty's journey is the thing that we all seek as human beings, a sense of certainty that our life's struggles are meaningful. Throughout the series then, Scotty will be faced with both the external dilemmas of the people he meets and the internal longing that he has to return to his former life.

Now let's talk about tone. In some ways tone is more about your overall voice as a writer than it is about each individual story you write, because as you develop you will naturally gravitate toward those subjects and genres you enjoy and are able to excel at. Just think about a few writers you admire. You like these writers as much for the way they tell their stories as the stories themselves. In other words, you like their voice, which grows out of the tone they infuse in their work over time, which in turn is something that you've come to expect from them. Yet each story they write also has its nuances and uniqueness. Taking time to describe the tone of each individual piece is a great way to understand the voice of the story you're working on, as well as help you define your overall voice as a writer. Here's how I did it for *Scotty's Travels:*

Tone:
The tone of the show is both dramatic and comedic as each week Scotty blindly stumbles into the travails of a stranger's life. The drama comes out of his efforts to help these people. The humor comes out of his "insanity," which we see from the inside out. That is, we see both the insane person wandering aimlessly, and the extraordinarily gifted person following the will of a higher power.

I like to think of it as TOUCHED BY AN ANGEL meets ONE FLEW OVER THE CUCKOO'S NEST. Or more affectionately, TOUCHED BY A LUNATIC.

As you can tell, the thing I've learned about my own voice over the years (and have consciously tried to develop) is that I am best suited to writing drama with little touches of humor. I'm not a comedy writer. To do comedy well, you really have to be able to write great jokes, and that's not me. My winning combination is a well-mixed cocktail of comedy and pathos, so I always try to inject humor wherever appropriate, and especially in places where the audience least expects it.

Then there's your cast of characters, which at this point is an absolutely essential piece of the puzzle because their motivations will determine where your story will lead. Your cast is your compass. If you truly know each and every one of these people well, you will never be lost; you will always have someone you can ask for directions along the way, which will definitely come in handy when that crisis moment inevitably hits. Here are the main characters in *Scotty's Travels:*

Characters:

Dr. Jonathon Scott – *Born and raised in a tough blue-collar town, it was always Scotty's dream to make a great living while helping those in need. Presently a prominent, 35-year-old psychiatrist, it appears that he's achieved that goal. But in his heart of hearts he knows it isn't true. The beautiful home, the fancy cars, the country club membership—it's all just a smoke screen for his inadequacy, a way of convincing himself that he's done enough. So when Liberty comes along and offers him a way to reconcile these feelings, it ultimately proves an offer he can't refuse. Now part messiah, part psychic, and part schizophrenic, Scotty is on a mission to truly heal the world—one person at a time.*

Liberty – Brutally forthright, frequently sarcastic, and always witty, Liberty is the ever-present voice in Scotty's head. Speaking with an English accent, she can be as authoritative as Margaret Thatcher or as whimsical as Mary Poppins. Scotty has no idea where she came from and, intriguingly, neither does she. Liberty is both his sidekick and his muse, his Tonto and his Obi-Wan Kenobi, albeit one that we never actually see.

George Lazarus – A well-polished, old-guard shrink in his 50s, George is Scotty's close friend and mentor. But upon witnessing Scotty's schizotypal behavior, George immediately turns from confidante to antagonist, insisting that Scotty undergo a psychiatric evaluation. George's character is an ominous presence throughout the series as the search for Scotty becomes a recurring theme.

Melissa Scott – Strong, vibrant, and intelligent, Melissa is the kind of woman who could run a Fortune 500 company, but still relishes being a full-time mom. She loves her husband deeply, but when he starts to flip out she is completely at a loss. Having met Scotty in her freshman year of college, she thought she knew all his eccentricities, but she never bargained for this.

Isabel Scott – 7-year-old Isabel possesses a maturity and an intelligence that is way beyond her years. She's both her father and her mother's daughter, already excelling both socially and academically.

Christopher Scott – *At this point, 4-year-old Christopher is 100% rough and tumble, and a startling mirror of the youthful innocent his father has, in many ways, reverted into.*

Finally, there's the story summary, which is basically a very abridged version of the next stage of the process, the outline.

Pilot Story Summary:
Following a session with a bipolar teenager, Scotty's feelings of professional inadequacy reach a zenith. Shortly afterward, Liberty visits him for the first time. Naturally, Liberty spooks Scotty, but when she inexplicably helps him foil the kid's attempted suicide, Scotty reconsiders the benefits of her presence and quickly warms to her.

Scotty tries to describe the miraculous experience to Melissa, but she has difficulty taking him seriously. Then, with Liberty's encouragement, Scotty inadvertently condemns the entire psychiatric profession in a speech to a packed convention house. The exhilaration he feels from speaking his mind eclipses any apprehension he might have had about sabotaging his career. This newfound freedom then spirals further out of control as he attempts to liquidate all his financial assets and take his family on the road. Frightened by the sudden irrational behavior, Melissa turns to George Lazarus for help. Together, George and Melissa make the painful decision to submit Scotty to a compulsory psychiatric evaluation.

Faced with the specter of being institutionalized for life, Scotty enlists Liberty's help, engineers a bold escape from the hospital, and sets out on his journey to heal the world.

One more important thing about Concept Documents before we move on . . .Generally, this is not a document that I show to anyone. It's mostly my way of working out all the various elements and internalizing them so I'm absolutely sure I know what the forest looks like before I start working on the trees. Still, it should be thorough and complete. Unlike the Notes Document, which is essentially a napkin sketch (and a messy one at that), when the Concept Document is done, it's a polished piece of work, usually somewhere between six and twelve pages long. This way, if at any point I do decide to share my story idea (usually with a producer or an agent), I now have a well-organized document that I can show anyone and feel comfortable doing so. The Concept Document is also important should I ever need to re-familiarize myself with the big picture.

The Outline

I remember the first day I arrived for orientation at the American Film Institute. There was a tremendous amount of consternation among the writers in the program because, other than the one hour per week we had as a group with our writing teacher, there really wasn't a whole lot scheduled for us. In fact, there was *nothing else* scheduled for us. By contrast, the producer, director, cinematographer, and production design students had all kinds of different classes they were required to take. Finally, someone asked the question: What exactly is it we're supposed to be doing here as writers? I'll never forget the somewhat befuddled expression on the face of the admissions director, who was sitting at the front of the room.

"Well," she said. "You write."

Like everyone else, I was a very green writer at that point and thought there was some magic bullet, some secret recipe for great writing, that I would now be privy to simply because I had been accepted into film school. The truth is, there really isn't. I would even go a step further and say that writing is one of those rare things in life that really *can't* be taught. You certainly need to acquire all the tools and techniques, attend all the lectures, seminars, and classes you can that identify the common ingredients found in good storytelling; but when it comes to actually preparing the meal, you pretty much have to develop your own recipe and simply start cooking. There's just no way around that.

This brings me back to the writer gene. Regardless of the medium in which you're working, if you are truly one of the writer brethren, you will never be intimidated by the countless hours you will have to spend educating yourself on the craft of writing, by having to be both teacher and student, and by all the sweat and toil it will take to tell your stories well. It'll never be easy, and nothing will test your mettle more than your next task, which is to write a good, solid outline.

The outline is the mechanism by which you assemble your story's structure, the key element that ultimately determines the quality of your work. Story structure is an extensive topic, one that has been explored by countless other authors, so to stay within the scope of this survival guide I will concentrate on a few fundamental outlining techniques that I use to structure my stories.

First, I study other works that are close in genre, tone, and structure to the story I'm telling. Yeah, I know. More research! It is more research, but it's a different kind of research than what I described earlier. This time I focus specifically on learning how other writers executed *their* stories —what they did well and what they did not so well—which means breaking those stories down, scene by scene, to expose the very bones of their structure.

Most of the original stories I write are speculative TV pilots and screenplays, so getting my hands on other writers' scripts, particularly ones that have actually been produced, is very important. The same thing is true if you're writing a novel, an interactive game, or any other type of written work. You have to study how other writers have done what you're now trying to do, and dissect their work rather meticulously in order to learn from them.

Next, I open a document in Final Draft (the screenwriting program most screenwriters use) and start writing down all the scenes I've already come up with in my Notes and Concept

Documents. At first, I don't worry so much about the order of the scenes. I just try to get them down on paper, and as I engage in this process, other potential scenes inevitably begin to emerge in my mind, and usually rather quickly. Though I don't yet formally write each scene with action and dialogue, as one does when writing a script, I do use a slug line for each (for example, EXT. DINING HALL – NIGHT) and then simply describe the scene's *content* as if I were explaining it to someone in conversation. Later, after I've compiled a fair amount of material, I start to work on the structuring (i.e., where each act breaks, and in which order the scenes belong).

In many cases I can tune in the entire story structure in this way, composing right on my computer, until I have conceived and described all the scenes in the story—which sounds awfully easy when you write it in a sentence like that, but in reality can be incredibly difficult and take weeks to get right. Other times I will use a white board or lay index cards out on a table, each with a single scene written on it, so I can continually rearrange them like pieces of a puzzle. Creative writers of all different stripes commonly use both of these approaches.

Another technique I use, either after I've got the whole structure worked out or when I'm still immersed in the outlining process, is to take out my trusty yellow pad and try to write down every scene in the script using just a single line for each. As you might imagine, this is yet another challenging task. You have to come up with a lot of very nifty shorthand, using as few words as possible to describe each scene, but what you end up with is your entire story structure on about one to two pages of the pad. This allows you to skim down the page imagining the entire story very quickly, scene by scene, from beginning to end. I've found this to be an excellent way to root out structural deficiencies, because when you're reading through it in fast-forward mode like this, any interruption in the natural flow of the story becomes much more glaring and apparent.

Everyone has different approaches to outlining. Some writers like to write very sparse outlines, providing just enough information to trigger the important elements of a scene in their mind when they write it later. Others like to deal with each scene in as much detail as they can up front. As you probably guessed, I'm in the second camp. I like to make tons of notes to myself right in the body of the outline and continue to flesh it out with as much background as I can. This often includes not just what is currently happening on the surface, but also the underlying thoughts, feelings, and motivations of the characters that drive each scene.

In other words, I continue to tune in the story, again, resisting the temptation to start turning it into a formal script for as long as possible, until it reaches the point that it's so well worked out and bloated with information that the only thing left to do is flesh out the action and write the dialogue.

SURVIVAL GUIDE SUMMARY

5. Tuning In the Radio

Things to Remember:

- All original stories exist in a perfect state as thought forms that are separate from you. Listen and tune them in like a radio signal.

- Begin with research. This is the soundest foundation you can set for your process.

- By taking the time to build a foundation of research, crisis moments are less likely to occur.

- Be a passive channel of information while you research, taking lots of notes without editing yourself. Let the ideas flow without judgment.

- Transcribe your notes at the end of your research period. Creating this Notes Document allows you to kick off your project without ever having to stare at a blank page.

- Create a Concept Document from your Notes Document. Avoid the temptation to rush into the outline or the first draft.

- Structure your story by writing the scenes on index cards or a whiteboard so you can view them as separate moments, rearranging them as necessary.

- Begin your outline by writing down all the scenes you have so far. Get all your ideas on the table without worrying about getting the story right. Your process will naturally fill in the blanks.

- Describe the scenes in your outline without actually writing them. Your outline is a road map, not the final product.

- Note deeper character motivations and other important story points in your outline. The deeper you dig, the more material you will have to work with.

- Once you've figured out most of your story structure, write all the scenes down on one or two pages of a legal pad, using one line for each scene, then skim the story to see if it flows.

Questions to Ask Yourself:

- What is the backdrop of your story and how can you learn more about it?

- Which websites will tell you more about your story's larger world and help you develop important details about your characters? Identify and print relevant materials. Bookmark the sites for future reference.

- Which books are available that will educate you about your story's world and its characters?

- Do you know anyone who is an expert in a field that will help you tell your story? If so, arrange to interview them and record their answers.

- How would you describe your story to someone in just a sentence or two? (Logline)

- What are you trying to say with this story? (Theme)

- What does the voice of the piece sound like? (Tone)

- Who inhabits this world? What are their backgrounds, flaws, hopes, and dreams? What compels them to do what they do? (Characters)

- What is your basic story? (Story Summary)

- What previously published or produced works are close in genre, tone, and structure to your story? Make a list, then study and breakdown those works.

6. This Draft's for You

Hallelujah! It's time to start writing. This is where all the hard work and patience in the beginning of the process finally pays off. Now that you've taken the time to research the subject of your story, clearly articulated what you want to say, and fully understand who your characters are, you can really begin to play and have fun within the world you've created. Even more importantly, because you've constructed an outline that's so rich in detail and depth that it's essentially a rough draft, you also don't have to worry that the whole damn thing will fall apart. In other words, you've successfully tuned in the radio and conceived this idea, this "child of your mind." Now its cells are starting to multiply!

To me, this is the most sacred part of the writing process, which is why I believe it's critical that you don't tell anyone—*not a single soul*—about this child that you're now carrying. Why?

Because this draft's for you.

Think about it. If you are essentially this story's "mother," if you're the one who's going to be charged with nurturing it, with protecting it, with being the best possible vessel you can be for it (for God-only-knows how many months or years), then damn it, why should you share it now, when it's so rife with possibilities and endless potential? What's the hurry? Why not take this opportunity to savor it a little bit before you expose it to the harsh, cruel world?

Like any expectant mother, you know it's going to be tough. You know there are going to be mornings when you don't feel so well, afternoons when you're going to pass out for no apparent reason, and days when you're tempted with strange cravings and inspirations. But you should also know that it's going to be okay, that all these things are simply part of the ride. Besides, there's no turning back now even if you wanted to, right? You're pregnant. Embrace it.

This is the juice of being a writer. This is as good as it gets, right here in the thick of this first draft. You've got to be fully conscious of this moment and know that this is what you do it for. You don't do it just to show off the finished product or to be recognized as some great genius or to get paid a lot of money. All of those things are nice, and I wish every writer in the world that kind of success, but at the end of the day that's not what writing is really about.

It's about the doing of it. That's the only part of it that's truly meaningful—the actual act of writing.

If you have the writer gene you know exactly what I'm talking about here, even if you won't (or can't) bring yourself to admit it. As writers, we're so full of passion and ambition. We have so much to say to the world, so many things we want to express, that we sometimes get caught up in this grand notion that the next script is the *one*; the next book is the *one*; the next great whatever is the *one*. But the truth is, it's the little moments of pleasure you receive along the way, the little successes that make it all worthwhile—writing a breakthrough scene or fixing a problematic line of dialogue or realizing that cutting a character will strengthen the whole piece, even when it's a character you're in love with. *Especially* when it's a character you're in love with.

Understanding and accepting this reality is so vital to your career. Why? Because no matter how much you've written in your life, you still have to start at square one each and every time. No two stories are the same, yet you will run into the same problems on story number one thousand that you ran into on story number one. Sure, some will come together easier than others, but you never get a free lunch. You still have to make each and every story work in its own unique way.

And what's the only thing that you can *really* count on through all this, the only thing that's consistent from one effort to the next? That's right, your process. *Your* process. Not the one that someone else has neatly laid out for you in a book about writing (including this one). The process that you've developed for yourself, the one that makes sense and works for *you*, the one that you will never enjoy more than when the story belongs *exclusively* to you. The one that you have no choice but to hone, refine, and love. That's where your gold is.

After all, if you're going to spend your entire life doing something day in and day out, year after year, you *better* love it. Otherwise what's the point?

Villains vs. Villainy

There's one particular storytelling element that is especially relevant to this discussion about keeping your original story to yourself while it incubates. It has to do with the tension or central conflict in a story, which frequently involves the presence of a villain.

It's often said, and I think quite correctly, that the best villains are the ones that aren't just evil, but are truly flawed human beings. While you clearly don't empathize with these characters in the same way that you do the hero of the story, you understand their motivation, and you can see why they've become such a powerful force of antagonism in the hero's world. In the case of theater, film, and television, if these villains are also portrayed by gifted actors as real, believable people, then their twisted, immoral agendas enhance the experience all the more.

In some stories though, there is no villain in the form of a person. The true villain is a thing, an idea, an emotion. Take *Romeo and Juliet*, for example. There are characters in the story that antagonize in various ways, but the real villain is the intolerance that exists between the two families, the *fear of the other*. It's this human failing, this overwhelming villainous force that conspires to ruin the happiness of the star-crossed lovers.

If you embrace this concept and start looking at every story through this lens, you quickly come to the conclusion that every hero's struggle is really a struggle against the underlying villainy, not the villain itself, even in stories where an actual human villain plays a clear and prominent role. In the hands of a talented writer, this character becomes a three-dimensional person, but really, it's just the personification of the conflict.

Where does this conflict come from then? What is the true source of this antagonism?

As I've already mentioned, I think you always need to be able to clearly articulate what you're writing about thematically. I think it's also important to be able to identify what it is in your own life that's inspiring you to tell a particular story at any given time. In other words:

How is your life experience shaping this work? What's going on in your life right now that you're struggling with? What villainy, past or present, are you personally trying to overcome?

When you can answer these questions, you've probably found the source of your main character's antagonism. Even if your main character is nothing like you, even if their background, their personality, and their circumstances are completely different than yours, even if they're not the same gender as you, their struggle is your struggle. This is another reason why it's so critical to keep the process to yourself in the early stages of development, to allow yourself to become more conscious of this relationship between you, your story, and your main character and to keep it free from outside interference.

We all have our demons to battle in life. The difference between us writers and everyone else in the world is that we're driven to battle them with words—which means that every story we tell is an exorcism on some level, a constructive way of emancipating ourselves of thoughts and feelings we couldn't possibly resolve in any other way.

Letting Go

Congratulations, you've finished your first draft. Woohoo! Guess what? Now it's time to let it go.

"What?" you say. "You just spent the last five pages telling me how important it is to keep this thing to myself, to nurture it, to savor it, to not tell another living soul about it, and now you expect me to let it go? Just like that?"

Yup. Here's why. Now that you're done with that first draft, this brainchild of yours is ready to be born. And just like a real live human child, from the moment you introduce it into the world, it's no longer just yours anymore. There's a whole host of other people who will immediately have an influence on it, beginning with the very first person who reads it. You have no choice but to cut the umbilical cord at some point. The only choice that remains is *when* to cut it. So always, always, always make sure you're 100% psychologically prepared before you do.

The key to this tricky piece of business is to remain humble and remember that this story exists separately from you, that it's a privilege to have been blessed with the gifts to tune it in and carry it to term. Your job now is to be the best steward you can be. Allow your story to be influenced by others, but also make sure the influence is positive and constructive and doesn't dilute the original intention or the core message you're trying to convey. It's never easy, but with the right frame of mind there's always a way to rise to this occasion.

For most writers, novices and veterans alike, this can be a pretty anxious time. It's worth noting, though not necessarily any more comforting, that storytelling has never been a one-way experience. From prehistoric campfires to the stages of Aeschylus and Molière, to the bright lights of Broadway and Hollywood, writers' works have always been shaped by the common culture. After all, that is your goal as a storyteller, right? You want to share your stories with the world—you want to let other people be a part of them, don't you?

Like it or not, at this point of the process, your story, like the millions that have come before it, now belongs to everyone. And the sooner you accept this fact, the better off both you and your story will be.

SURVIVAL GUIDE SUMMARY

6. This Draft's for You

Things to Remember:

- Don't share your original story with anyone before you've written your first draft. Let it develop free from outside influence.

- The real reason you write is to experience the joy of expressing yourself. Never lose touch with this simple fact.

- No matter how much you've written in your life you must still start at square one each time, and make each story work in its own unique way.

- Every story you write is an exorcism, a way of freeing yourself from thoughts or feelings you can't quite resolve any other way.

- The moment you give your script to someone else to read, you have given it to the world. There is no turning back.

Questions to Ask Yourself:

- How is your life experience shaping this work? What's going on in your life right now that you're struggling with? What villainy, past or present, are you personally trying to overcome?

- How can you infuse the struggles of your personal life into your story's main conflict? How can you infuse them into your main character?

- Have you done absolutely everything with your first draft that you set out to do? Don't leave any stone unturned.

- Are you 100% sure that you're ready to give your script to someone for feedback? Are you truly ready to let it be shaped by the common culture?

7. The Art of Giving Notes

You may be wondering why I've decided to include a chapter on *giving* script notes in this survival guide, as well as why I've chosen to place it before the chapter on *receiving* script notes. To be honest with you, I spent a lot of time thinking about this myself, and the conclusion I finally reached was this:

If you understand how to give a good note to another writer, then you will have a much better understanding of what to do with a note, good or bad, when you receive one.

I have to admit that part of me is also writing this chapter for all those producers, executives, editors, dramaturges, agents, and anyone else out there whose job involves giving notes to creative writers. If I can shed any light on the writer's psyche with respect to this process, and give you folks a few pointers as to how to be more effective, then that would be yet another proud feather in my cap.

Have a Constructive Attitude

To say that you should always give constructive criticism to another writer is kind of like saying that you need to brush your teeth every day. It's the healthy thing to do (for both of you).

According to my dictionary, the definition of *constructive* is "to serve a useful purpose" or "to build up." This means that as the person giving notes you have to do more than just identify problems. You have to offer ideas for potential solutions. You have to actually *be* constructive.

Remember, you are trying to help another writer tell a story as best as *they* can. So first and foremost, you need to make that writer feel that you're on their team, that you are right there beside them on this construction project, wearing a hard hat—not just some pencil pusher who doesn't want to get his or her hands dirty. Nothing will help you prove this to the writer more than if you bring concrete ideas to the table, even if those ideas don't quite work perfectly. It's the fact that you've taken the time to try and come up with something—anything— that the writer can *actually use* that makes the difference.

This is sound advice when giving notes to any type of artist, but when it comes to creative writing it carries even more weight, because unlike drawing or painting, composing music, making computer animation, or working in almost any other art form, the basic skill set— writing—is something that everyone has.

Everyone knows how to put a sentence together (presumably), whether you're a professional writer or not. And everyone has a certain visceral understanding of storytelling. This perception of *common competence*—that anyone can be a qualified note giver because *everyone* knows how to write—makes having a constructive attitude and letting that attitude inform the notes just as significant as the very substance of them.

This is especially important when you're giving notes to a writer who is somewhat green. If the work clearly has a lot of issues, you'll need to exercise a little restraint. Please don't get into *all* the problems, as much as you would like to. Just find something positive to say about their idea, give them a few things to chew on that will help them take baby steps toward improving it, and leave them with a sense of excitement about the road ahead. Like novices in any other line of work, novice writers need encouragement more than anything else. You just have to allow them to develop and trust their writer genes to do the rest.

Have Some Humility

This is a biggie. It's so much easier to recognize the flaws in other people's work than it is to recognize them in our own. As a result, sometimes when you read another writer's story or script, whether you're aware of it or not, you suddenly become filled with this false sense of superiority, this lethal dose of misguided power, as if you're some omnipotent writer-god who has all the answers.

Why does this happen? First of all, you have the advantage of having fresh eyes. You haven't been trying to tell this story for months and months. Second, because you're not down there on the ground trying to build the damn thing brick by brick, you also have the benefit of sitting back and looking at it from a five-thousand-foot point of view. No wonder you feel like a god! So here's your chance to throw a few lightning bolts at the mere mortal who's made the mistake of asking you for help, right? Do me a favor, don't be that guy. Always give notes with empathy and humility, and remember, the next time it will be you on the other end of that lightning bolt.

Giving notes with humility also means resisting the temptation to *take ownership* of the other writer's story. You need to be careful not to come off sounding like a know-it-all; you can't give the other writer the impression that you think you can do a better job with their idea than they can. Again, you're there to *help*, not rewrite the story. Not that you shouldn't have strong opinions. Strong opinions are good, but your objective must be to lead the writer in a direction that will yield positive results, not force them to come around to your line of thinking. You can't help them unless they trust you, and if they feel their story is being hijacked or they're being jerked around, they will not trust you.

Focus on the Big Idea

The legendary writer/director John Huston once said: "A good screenplay is like a bell. When you ring it, every scene in it reverberates with the theme of the story." I have always loved this concept, not only because it so eloquently sums up a very universal truth about writing, but because it also applies to note giving so well. The more you can focus your notes on issues that speak directly to a story's core message, the greater the impact you will have on the writer's next draft. Not that this is an easy thing to do. Which brings me to another important point:

Giving good notes takes work.

When another writer asks you to read their story and you accept, you now have a responsibility to spend the time and effort it takes to not just read it, but to *think deeply* about it. You have made a covenant with the writer, so you owe it to them to give your honest and most well-considered opinions. If you don't think you have the time or the energy to do so, my advice is to be honest and just tell the writer flat out that you can't read right now. The writer may be a little miffed, but not half as upset as they will be when you finally get around to phoning in your feedback.

Assuming you've made the commitment, the best way to start is to read the script or story through more than once, make notes to yourself, and then ask yourself the question: What is this writer trying to say with this work? If the message is unclear, then that's your first note to the writer. Start by simply engaging the writer in a discussion at this very high level.

Next, I always try to find no more than three things the writer can address that speak directly to the theme of the piece or at least to some major aspect of it—big things that "reverberate," as John Huston said. Try to make these notes as specific and executable as possible, and again, try not to give more than three of them. In fact, sometimes one razor-sharp thought that cuts right to the heart of the thing is all that's needed to illuminate a whole new world of possibilities.

For example, in one of my spec television pilots, the first scene involves the main character arriving home after disappearing for three years, only to find the woman who was once his fiancée in bed with another man. This other man is now her husband. The main character has been missing for years and has a severe case of posttraumatic amnesia, which means there is a donut hole in his memory, so he doesn't even remember how or when he went missing. I thought I was pretty clever beginning the story this way, but the note I received was that rather than strengthening the scene with a degree of shock value, catching the fiancée and her new husband having sex actually seemed to distract from the main character's real dilemma.

Thematically, the story is about a man struggling to reclaim his identity, so when I removed the sex, the scene was suddenly able to breathe and took on a much deeper sense of delirium. This proved to be a significantly better approach. Why? Because now I was striking directly at the heart of my story, which speaks to the struggle we all face in a world that often confuses and conspires against us.

The note giver in this case didn't tell me *how* to execute the rewrite. They merely pointed out a weakness (i.e., catching them having sex seems to cheapen the main character's dilemma) and suggested a different approach. "What if he came home and learned his fiancée had married this other guy, but in a different context?" the note giver said. They understood what I was after with the piece as a whole and gave me a very specific, executable note that, sure enough, ended up reverberating throughout the entire script.

Focus on Structure and Character

In addition to focusing on the big idea, there are two other ways of framing your notes that I have found to be very productive.

One way is to give notes that specifically address the structure of the story. If a story isn't working, you can almost always trace the problem back to an element that hasn't been adequately set up or an important piece of information that is missing, not allowing something else to pay off later. So as you read the piece, flag the areas where something feels off. Then go back later and try to identify the scene or the moment earlier in the story that appears to be connected to the off-kilter moment you flagged. Most of the time the setup is there, it's just not executed well enough. Other times, if the writer is really lost, it will be entirely AWOL. Either way, looking at the story in terms of both setups and payoffs can be a pretty effective approach.

Another good way to frame your notes is to focus on the characters and their motivations, because even the most plot-driven stories need characters whose actions continue to move the story toward its logical and inevitable conclusion. Does the behavior of a particular character make sense for the situation? What does the character want in a particular scene? What does the character want from the other characters in the story? What do the various characters want on a deeper, subconscious level? All these questions are helpful in giving good notes because, again, they start to drill into the core message of the story.

Another benefit of going the character route is that all writers fall in love with their characters and generally don't feel threatened by discussions about them. In fact, they usually welcome these kinds of discussions. If you're a writer yourself, I'm sure you can relate to this. And if you're a non-writing note giver, there's probably no better way to earn a writer's trust than establishing that you've put some thought into these people who have been inhabiting the writer's mind twenty-four hours a day. Either way, if you come at it from this angle you're not only bound to find yourself in a pretty interesting conversation, you'll also be more likely to get the writer to be receptive to some of your more challenging notes.

SURVIVAL GUIDE SUMMARY

7. The Art of Giving Notes

Things to Remember:

- If you understand how to give good notes to another writer, you will have a much better understanding of what to do with notes, good or bad, when you receive them.

- Have a constructive attitude when giving notes to another writer. Make them feel that you are on their team.

- Always offer concrete ideas that writers can potentially use to improve their story. Don't just identify problems.

- All writers need encouragement more than anything else, especially writers who are just starting out.

- It's always easier to see flaws in other writers' work than it is to see them in your own. Have some empathy and some humility.

- Giving good notes on a story takes work. Make sure you're committed before you agree to take the plunge.

- Focus your notes on the "big idea" of the writer's story.

- Focus your notes on the writer's setups and payoffs.

- Focus your notes on the writer's characters.

Questions to Ask Yourself:

- What is the writer trying to say? Is the message clear? If not, this is a great place to begin your note-giving process.

- What are the three most salient notes that you can give that "reverberate" with the theme of the writer's work?

- If a moment in the writer's story isn't working, is there a moment earlier in the narrative that didn't quite set it up adequately? Chances are, there is.

- Does the behavior of each character make sense for the situation?

- What does each character want in each scene?

- What does each character want from the other characters in the story?

- What does each character want on a deeper, subconscious level?

8. The Art of Receiving Notes

You've finished your first draft, the one that was just for you. Mazel tov. Are you ready for some feedback? I hope so, because ready or not here it comes.

The most important thing you need to do now is:

Keep an open mind.

Remember, you're not pregnant with the child anymore. The child is here in the world with us and soon it will have babysitters, teachers, grandparents, siblings, friends, and all sorts of other people who will start to exert a sway over it. As I said before, your job now is to be a sure-handed guide, to *receive* the advice and insight of others, to make level-headed decisions about your story's future, and to continue to shape it into the story it wants to become.

Does this mean that you're no longer in control of the process? Absolutely not. On the contrary, your process is more important than ever. What it means is that you have to find a way to be comfortable with the fact that no matter who you give your script to, from this day forward it will always be seen in an imperfect light. No matter what you do with the notes you receive, no matter how hard you try, no matter how many painstaking times you rewrite it, there will always be another person with another opinion, and there will always be more notes.

Seriously. Always.

Are you starting to understand now why I was so emphatic about loving and cherishing the time you spent writing that first draft—when the idea belonged to no one else but you?

Again, I'm not saying you should just throw up your hands and jump off a bridge. What I'm saying is you have to be super cognizant of the fact that you've now entered an entirely new phase in the life of your story, one in which you've got to make a substantial attitude adjustment as you approach the work ahead. So don't worry, it's not all doom and gloom. In fact, there's definitely another way of looking at this next step with the glass half full.

The Story Will Never Stop Being Told

When you started this grand adventure, you had nothing more than a passing notion, a faint, undefined radio signal, right? Then you started to tune that radio signal in and it got clearer. Then its cells started to multiply and miraculously it grew into this fleshed out, three-dimensional being. But that doesn't mean it's not *still* growing and changing. As a matter of fact it will *never* stop growing and changing. In other words:

The story will never stop being told.

If you can genuinely buy into this concept, then you will always be able to remain open to new ideas, and no note will ever freak you out. Okay, I take that back. Of course there will be notes that freak you out, but there will never be a note that takes you by surprise, or makes you want to jump off that bridge because you feel it threatens the precious sanctity of your creation. You'll be egoless about it (if that's possible), and at peace with the fact that not only does this story exist outside of you, it also exists in a state of constant change. So actually, you're still tuning in that radio, and you always will be—because the story will *never* really be done. There will *never* be a final draft, and there's absolutely *nothing* precious about it but your core message.

Another very memorable moment from my film school days illustrates what I'm talking about here in perhaps the simplest of ways. The wonderful writer/director and prolific producer James L. Brooks came to speak to us one afternoon, and part of the discussion involved screening selected scenes from his films and television shows. After they showed a scene from the Academy Award winning *Terms of*

Endearment someone asked a question, but the pensive Brooks didn't answer for several long moments. He just kept staring at the screen, until finally he explained that he couldn't help thinking that he should have cut away from Jack Nicholson's character earlier in the scene to capture a little more of Shirley MacLaine's reaction.

I found this absolutely fascinating. Here it was 1989, a full six years after the film had been released, probably at least ten or more since he first began working on the idea, and who knows how long since he last looked at that particular scene. Now he's in this auditorium full of adoring film students showering him with praise about his work. You'd think he'd just sit back and enjoy the ride, right? Wrong. His writer gene wouldn't let him. Instead, he gets right back in there and keeps editing, keeps tuning in the story, keeps rewriting the script in his mind.

Clearly this is a guy who is well aware that the story never stops being told.

Mining for Gold

Another healthy way to look at the note-receiving process is to see it as a gold-mining expedition, an opportunity to discover nuggets of wisdom that will help make your story better, as opposed to an encounter with a nuclear submarine that's about to blow it to smithereens.

In order to be a successful gold miner though, you have to dig—and you have to dig persistently. You can't be passive. You have to be proactive.

But how can you be proactive when you're the one receiving the notes, when you're the one who's supposed to be doing the *listening*?

Here's the deal: When someone gives you notes you need to be open and respectful and consider each one carefully, but at the same time you can't let the note giver get away with being an omnipotent authority on your story, or let them poke holes in it without offering anything constructive (as we discussed in the previous chapter). It's your work. You know it better than anyone, and you know what you're trying to say with it. If you think a note has some validity, use the conversation to drill deeper into it. *Shape* the note into something that can help you realize your vision by getting more specifics out of your note giver. By asking them follow-up questions, you guide the direction of the discussion and engage them in the process, which will show them you value their opinion—and if they know you value their opinion, you will definitely get more out of them. Through this exchange, you will automatically begin to collate the *useable* notes in your mind and incorporate them into the tuning process, even if you're not entirely sure how you'll apply them.

On the other hand, if you don't think a note is valuable, then don't spend any time on it. Let it go. *Immediately.* Whatever you do, don't get into a discussion as to why a note is an affront to you or your story. Being defensive about anything during this conversation is a complete waste of time. If you determine that a note doesn't work for you, just forget it and move on. It's not important. There's too much gold in them thar hills.

The Note Beneath the Note

Sometimes even the most experienced note givers aren't always conscious of the note they're actually giving you. They point out a problem and make a genuine effort to give you a possible solution, but they just can't quite articulate it. Or the note is only marginally valid—or even worse, completely off base—and they haven't got a clue. Either way, it isn't helpful. But you can tell from their sincerity that what they're saying isn't entirely trivial either. So the real question is:

What's their intuition trying to tell you? What is the note beneath the note?

Very often I find the key to this little riddle doesn't quite reveal itself until I've received a few sets of notes from multiple people. At that point, the same note (or several notes that are similar) will have probably appeared over and over again, which eventually unmasks the underlying issue and makes it fairly obvious. But more often than not there's something else that all this feedback triggers, a more subliminal, organic answer to a deeper problem that I knew was there all along but couldn't quite solve or articulate on my own.

It's not unusual for this note beneath the note to end up being the most valuable of all. So instead of dismissing that weird moment in the conversation when both you and your note giver seem to be a little lost, pay extra close attention. That moment might turn out to be far more helpful and instructive than you think.

Choose Your Note Givers Wisely

One of the first jobs I had after I got out of film school was working for a very successful television producer by the name of Mort Lachman. Mort was about seventy-two years old at the time and was the sweetest guy in the world. He had started out his career as a joke writer for Bob Hope, then after years of doing USO shows and TV specials in the 1940s, '50s, and '60s, went on to produce sitcoms for Norman Lear in the '70s and '80s: *All In The Family, Kate and Allie, Gimme A Break*, among many others.

I used to pick Mort up at his house every morning and drive him to the studio, so I got to know him pretty well, which was a true gift. Between all the fun stories and anecdotes he would tell me, he also gave me lots of sage advice, the greatest piece of which came after I finally worked up the nerve to ask him to read one of my scripts.

"I'd be happy to," he said. "As long as you understand that my opinion doesn't mean a damn thing."

I was of course quite confused by this.

"The only opinion that matters," he then said with that characteristic twinkle in his eye, "is the opinion of the person who's saying 'yes.'"

Translation: If someone wants to buy your script, what difference does it make what anyone else thinks? The buyer is ultimately the only one you have to please.

This is very true, and the more I've written over the years, the more I've realized this principle actually speaks to an even broader question:

How invested in your success is this person giving you notes?

In the case where the note giver is paying you actual cash money the answer is obviously "very invested." But there are also other degrees of investment to consider. Is the note giver a producer you're working with who is putting their own time into helping you develop the script so they can be attached to produce it? Does the note giver work for the publisher you're trying to get a book deal with or an agent who represents you? In all these cases, there's obviously a potential financial reward for the other party in return for their investment.

Is the note giver another writer? If so, are they a close friend, someone who truly wants to see you succeed, or are they just an acquaintance who may not care that much? Do they take the note-giving process as seriously as you do? If they do, then you've found a valuable relationship to cultivate. If not, it won't take you long to find out.

There's also the "casting" of your note givers. In other words, does this person's sensibility match the material that you want them to read? As close as you are with your buddy the horror writer, you really don't want to ask him to critique your sitcom, unless he's an equally talented comedy writer. This may be even more important when it comes to non-writing note givers, because unlike those of us with the writer gene, their *taste* in material tends to influence their opinions a little more than the nuts-and-bolts mechanics of the writing. Not that any given note giver, writer, or non-writer can't be effective across a wide range of genres. As discussed in the previous chapter, all note givers have their strengths and their weaknesses.

The important point here is that it's smart to establish a wide variety of note givers you can draw on, who are well-suited to read your work, and to tap into those various resources to get a nice spectrum of feedback on each and every piece you write.

Don't Sweat the Small Stuff

Important as it is for the note giver to trust the writer to digest the big picture notes and be able to make hay with them, it's equally important for the writer to be able to identify and dismiss the smaller, less significant notes that will likely get swallowed up in the rewriting process.

This means with every note you receive, you need to ask yourself:

Can I use this idea to make my story better and does it support my core message?

If the answer to this question is yes, then your mission is clear. You have to find a way to incorporate this note into your next draft. If the answer is no, well, *hasta la vista, baby*.

Obviously this is another one of those things that's a hell of a lot easier to write in a book than it is to actually *do*. Believe me, it will never be that cut-and-dry. *Never*. But that's why God gave you the writer gene. It's your job to separate the cream from the rest of the crop and then figure out what to do with it.

Once you understand how the success of each draft, and each work as a whole, hinges on this delicate dance between note giver and note receiver, not only will the quality of your stories improve, but you're ability to crank out those drafts with increasing proficiency will improve as well.

SURVIVAL GUIDE SUMMARY

8. The Art of Receiving Notes

Things to Remember:

- Keep an open mind.

- Your story will never stop being told and is in a constant state of change.

- There is nothing precious about your story but its core message.

- Shape the notes you receive by asking follow-up questions and getting more specifics out of your note givers. *Mine for gold.*

- Always value your note givers' opinions.

- Ignore the notes you don't think are useable. Don't waste time arguing about them.

- Choose your note givers wisely, according to their strengths and taste in material.

Questions to Ask Yourself:

- Which notes apply to the core message of your story and which apply to specific details?

- Which notes support your core message? Which ones don't?

- What follow-up questions can you ask that will help shape the notes into usable ideas?

- Are any of the notes from multiple note givers the same? Chances are those notes are valid.

- Are there any notes that felt right but that your note giver couldn't quite articulate? What was their intuition trying to tell you? What was the note beneath their note?

- How invested in your success is your note giver?

9. The Art of Executing Notes

I grew up on Long Island about an hour east of New York City, so when I first graduated from college and decided I wanted to pursue a career in the entertainment business, the most logical thing to do was hop on the Long Island Railroad and trek into the Big Apple to see what opportunities I could drum up. In those days I was also very interested in being an actor as well as a writer, so I began taking classes at The Lee Strasberg Creative Center downtown. Funny enough, it wasn't too long after I started studying there that one of the teachers became interested in a play I'd written. This teacher was a working actor himself, and there happened to be a good role for him in the piece, so it was a perfect storm. He got himself a showcase and at the ripe old age of twenty-two I had my first production!

Now, it's important for you to understand the context of this story. This was actually *before* I had gone off to film school, so I was even wetter behind the ears than I was when I arrived in Los Angeles a year or so later. In fact, this was only the second time I had even attempted to write a script of any kind. Therein lies the beauty of the writer gene. I had no earthly idea what the hell I was doing, and yet, just as I had done with my "Triplets" masterpiece when I was just a tyke, somehow I made it work. The problem, I soon discovered, was:

The writer gene can only take you so far.

I'll never forget the conversation I had with the director one night toward the end of the run. He was a very cantankerous guy with a few *personal issues*, so no conversation with him could ever have been mistaken as pleasant. This one, however, was like getting doused with a bucket of ice water, as he proceeded to go on about a thirty-minute tirade, berating me for how I had failed miserably as a writer because I hadn't adequately reworked the play during the rehearsal period. What made this moment so ironic and so incredibly confusing to me was the constant roar of laughter and applause that could be heard coming from the house the entire time he went on his rant. Not to mention the fact that pretty much everything else about the experience had been fantastic. In a ridiculously short amount of time, I had gotten someone to produce my play. A month or two later there were actors coming in, saying my words in auditions. Then we were in rehearsals. And then the audiences *loved* it. Well, enough of them at least for me to feel a significant sense of satisfaction and accomplishment.

Yet that cranky freakin' director was 100% right. It could have been better. A *lot* better. In fact, to be honest, while the theme and structure of the play were strong, it was a pretty raw piece of work in many ways, written by a very raw writer. If I were to reread it now, God forbid, I'm sure that I would absolutely shudder at the characters' lack of depth and the stiffness of some of the dialogue, which even then I secretly had some discomfort about.

So why didn't I just rewrite it during rehearsals like any normal playwright would? The short and simple answer is: *I didn't know how.* I was so green that I didn't even know when the director was giving me a note, much less how to execute one.

Fortunately, I've learned a thing or two since then and have developed what I think is a pretty sound approach to the revision process—which, by the way, isn't all that different from the process of creating a first draft. The only real difference is that other people have now weighed in, so to some degree you're reacting to their opinions. But the actual writing process, the mechanics of making the story work once you re-engage in it, is pretty much the same. The trick is to get your mind right first.

The Note Giver Has Left the Building

So, you've sorted through all the notes you've received on your script and determined which ones are useful and which ones aren't. Now it's time to show the note giver the door. You can't ever have anyone else's voice bouncing around in your head when you're writing. You must have an absolutely clear channel so you can get back to the business of tuning in your story. Besides, your note giver has helped you all they can up until this point. You shouldn't feel bad about tuning *them* out.

In a similar vein, you can't do a rewrite trying to anticipate what that note giver will say next. This can be especially problematic when you're getting paid to write what you're working on, or when the note giver is highly invested in your success. In the end, like you, all they really want is for the work to be better, so it really doesn't matter what they think until they actually tell you.

Now here's the good news:

Note givers have short memories.

When your note giver reads your new draft, they're going to have a whole new set of notes. Ideally, with each passing draft there will be less and less, but even if there's still a lot of work to be done, your note giver is always going to be commenting on what's in front of them, not what you did before.

Keep your focus. Get back to your process. And remember, the note giver has left the building.

Major vs. Minor Revisions

The next piece of business you need to handle is to determine the scope of the rewrite you're about to do. Is it a major revision or a minor one?

A major revision means making significant changes to the structure of the story. So, in addition to potentially adjusting characters, changing the content of scenes, and rewriting dialogue, various scenes may need to be reordered and/or replaced and entire acts reconfigured.

A minor rewrite may involve adding or removing selected scenes, but doesn't involve such a widespread overhaul. It mostly entails revising action and dialogue within the existing structure.

There are two big reasons why it's important to make this distinction. First, you've got to understand what you're getting yourself into, and how much of your time and energy it's going to require. I'm not suggesting you rush or change your process, but to be a professional you do have to develop an accurate sense of your own limitations, while being able to consistently and reliably *bring the ship into port.*

Second, when you're getting paid to write something, the one question your employer will inevitably ask is:

How long do you think this revision is going to take?

If you're getting paid a flat fee for the work, your answer is mostly about giving them the product in a reasonable time frame. But if you're getting paid on a weekly, daily, or hourly rate, then this is also a financial question. So, it's obviously critical (for both you and your employer) that you have a firm grasp on the speed with which you feel you can execute.

Minor rewrites are not particularly taxing. Major rewrites, on the other hand, can be very difficult and usually entail going back to the whiteboard and/or index cards to rejigger the scenes in order to satisfy the notes. What's especially unnerving about this is that the notes often don't call for the entire story to be trashed, but when you start to replace just a scene or two, it's like pulling a loose thread on your sweater. Before you know it, the whole thing unravels. So, it's not uncommon for what starts out to be a minor rewrite to turn into a major one.

It's also often hard to part with certain scenes. Not necessarily because you're in love with them (though that also happens), but because they're actually *working*. The problem is they don't work *anymore* because of the new direction the story is taking.

Psychologically, the way to deal with this is to try and get yourself into that same mindset of "letting go" you adopted between finishing the first draft and giving it to people for feedback. The same way that the child was suddenly no longer just *your* baby, it's now no longer just your baby *again*. So be prepared to let go of *everything* about it if you have to.

On a more technical note, something that I often do at this point is use a *double-yellow-pad approach*. Remember my outlining process in which I write every scene on a single line so I can skim the entire story in fast-forward-mode? I do the same thing again, only this time I do it twice, on two separate yellow pads. On the first pad I write down the current structure (based on the current draft). On the second pad I restructure the story, this time allowing myself to embellish the scenes wherever necessary (in other words, not restricting myself to one line per scene). By studying the structure of my current draft on the first pad, I'm able to recognize various components that are working and use them as templates to reinvent setups and payoffs within the new structure I'm assembling on the second pad. Then, when I've got the new structure worked out, I once again write the whole thing down, using one scene per line so that I can see if it passes the fast-forward test.

Once you make it through this gauntlet, you'll discover that on a high level, the structure is similar and the core message remains unchanged, but since some of the content is different, the story is expressed in a whole new way. Again, this is because the story exists separately from you. You have merely taken another run at tuning in the radio and brought the signal through a little clearer this time.

The key is to be just as patient as you were with the first draft. You don't want to jump back in too soon and start formally composing the scenes until you feel absolutely confident with the new structure.

Make Your Battle Plan

Now it's time to apply this new structure. I approach this part of the process by opening the script document in Final Draft and making notes within each scene using a different color font (leaving the text of the original scene intact for the moment). This is similar to the process of creating the original outline, only now I frame my descriptions of each scene a little differently. Instead of describing the content, I explain to myself what has to be done with each scene as I move forward with the rewrite. Basically, I'm writing myself an instruction manual—or as I like to think of it, a *battle plan*.

Here's a hypothetical example:

INT. DINER (page 10)
This scene stays the same as the previous draft. Dan still meets Lucy at the diner.

INT. LUCY'S APARTMENT (page 30)
This scene is essentially the same as the previous draft, except instead of blurting out: "Will you marry me?" and then having second thoughts about it, the moment the words leave Dan's lips, he hesitates—which makes it obvious to Lucy that he's having second thoughts and ruins the entire evening. Lucy leaves, pissed.

INT. LUCY'S APT. BLDG. – HALLWAY (page 35)
Insert a new scene here where Dan leaves a yellow rose at the foot of Lucy's door.

> *EXT. AMUSEMENT PARK (page 50)*
> *Adjust this scene per the earlier notes.*
> *Instead of making this the scene where*
> *Lucy loses the ring, this is now the*
> *"make-up" scene. Put it on the street in*
> *front of Lucy's apartment instead of at*
> *the amusement park. Or maybe put it*
> *in the diner where she and Dan first*
> *met?*

You see how I asked myself a question there in that last note? You don't have to have all the answers at this point. You just have to give yourself a pretty clear idea of what needs to be done so you have something to lean on later when you come back to write the scene in earnest. You also don't need to worry quite as much about the details of scenes that come later, because those scenes will inevitably be affected by how the earlier ones turn out. Not that you shouldn't have a solid plan for them. Just keep in mind that those later scenes are the ones that will most likely deviate from the plan, so remain flexible.

If you're getting paid to write the script or if your note giver is highly invested in your development of it, you may also want to consider giving them the battle plan *before* you actually execute the rewrite. What this does is show them the scene-by-scene detail of what they will see in the revised draft. This can be a very valuable way to avoid miscommunication with an employer, because if they sign off on the battle plan, chances are pretty good they'll like the rewrite. On the other hand, if they have more notes after they see the battle plan, then you have just saved yourself an enormous amount of time, because it's a hell of a lot easier to revise the plan than it is to revise the rewritten script.

Remember, the goal here is to raise the level of the work with each successive note session, to tune that radio signal in clearer and clearer so that your story eventually comes as close as it possibly can to that pure, perfect form in your mind. That doesn't mean you can't make a successful sharp, ninety-degree turn at any point along the way. Just be sure to always fall back on your process, create that sound battle plan, and always be mindful to keep the main thrust of the effort consistent with your core message.

SURVIVAL GUIDE SUMMARY

9. The Art of Executing Notes

Things to Remember:

- Once you're ready to start your rewrite, it's time to tune out your note giver. *The note giver has left the building*.

- A major revision means there are significant changes that need to be made to the structure of the story.

- A minor revision may involve adding or removing selected scenes, but mostly entails revising action and dialogue within the existing structure.

- Don't be afraid to go back to the white board or the index cards to execute your rewrite.

- Be prepared to let go of every scene.

- Use a double-yellow-pad approach, writing down the current structure on one pad, and the new one on another.

- Be patient. Don't start composing the new scenes until you're absolutely confident with the new structure.

- Once you have your new structure, make a battle plan, describing within the body of your script how you are going to modify each scene.

- Consider giving your note giver the battle plan for more notes before executing the rewrite.

Questions to Ask Yourself:

- What is the scope of your rewrite? Is it a major or a minor one?

- How long do you think your rewrite is going to take? Make an estimate and see how accurate you are.

- Are there components (individual scenes or sequences) of your old structure you can use as templates for parts of your new structure?

- Is each modification you're making consistent with your core message?

10. Writing Partners

Being in a writing partnership is kind of like being in a marriage. It's an intimate relationship that needs to be based on trust, mutual respect, and commitment. You have to *really* like this other person with whom you'll be spending a great deal of time and sharing your ideas and your dreams. So if having a writing partner is one relationship too many in your life, you have my permission to stop reading this chapter right now and skip to the next one—or forever hold your peace!

Assuming I haven't scared you away, let's talk about those three things I just mentioned…

Trust, in this relationship, means that no idea is a bad idea—that you can throw anything out there no matter how lame it might sound, and there will never be any judgment about it on the part of the other writer. It means that this person will always have your back creatively.

Mutual respect means that you never trash each other's work. I learned this lesson the hard way when a writer I was working with repeatedly deleted or radically rewrote scenes that I had written in *our* script without even thinking about discussing the changes with me first. You can imagine how that partnership turned out.

Commitment means always being willing to do what it takes to make the work better, and always seeing the job through until it's done. This is the toughest one of all, because as I've already mentioned, the story never stops being told. So no script is really ever done—which means, like parents, once you conceive and give birth to these *mind children*, they connect the two of you forever.

What You Need to Give Up

When you enter into this relationship, the first thing you have to be willing to give up is creative ownership of the work. When you work with a writing partner, there is no draft just for you. In fact, there is no *you* anymore. *You* are now *we.* So every idea, every outline, every script, right from the very outset, is only fifty percent yours, creatively speaking. (To be clear, I'm not in any way referring to ownership in the financial sense here. Obviously that's an entirely different conversation.)

The second thing you have to be willing to give up is creative autonomy. Since fifty percent of the work belongs to you and the other fifty percent belongs to your partner, you are only one of two votes that determine every creative decision that must be made on its behalf. So everything must be discussed at some point and negotiated if necessary, which can sometimes be a sticky business.

Most significantly, you also have to be willing to give up your own voice, as does your partner, for the sake of this third, entirely unique creature that is the product of your collaboration. This may seem like a scary proposition, effectively losing your identity as an individual writer (and make no mistake, that's exactly what it is), but in my experience, this melding of voices is actually one of the coolest aspects of writing with partners—the fact that you're creating something that would never be the same if it were written by any two other people.

What You Gain

Here are the big advantages to writing with a partner. First of all, you get a second brain, and who couldn't use one of those, right? Just think about all those painstaking hours you need to spend tuning in the radio, carving out characters that are properly motivated, endlessly structuring and restructuring. Now you don't have to figure out all that stuff on your own. Half the answers are your partner's responsibility.

Plus, now you have a reliable sounding board to help work through all the rough patches, a person who's as knee-deep in the story as you are and equally invested in making it work.

You're now also working with someone who is not only responsible for half the ideas, but half the workload as well. In reality, nothing ever shakes out exactly even, but if there's good communication between the parties, clearly defined expectations, and a sincere work ethic, you'll be well on your way to doing some great things together.

The Partner Process

Like the process you create for yourself, the process you develop with a writing partner needs to emerge organically over time. Almost all of the collaborations that I've had with other writers have begun with simple conversations, sometimes accidentally, where we both found ourselves intrigued by a specific idea or a mutual area of interest. In some cases, one of us may have already written down some notes on the subject or done some high-level brainstorming, but generally it's best to pretty much start from scratch.

That first conversation usually turns into a series of conversations, during which time we also separately do a little homework. This research period tends to be less intense than the one I described earlier, because in addition to sharing the workload, the knowledge gap also seems to close a lot faster when two people bring their life experiences and their collective energy to the table as opposed to just one.

When we get to the Concept Document phase, my preference is to continue working together in the same room, possibly with a white board, while we further define all the high-level aspects of the story. Then one of us can go off and transcribe the notes and begin to write up the document, which we can then pass back and forth, editing until we're happy with it.

At this point, it is still preferable to be in the same room so we can work on the structure and lay the foundation for the outline together. Otherwise, one partner tends to do more of the heavy lifting on the story than the other, which skews the creative equation a little too much in one person's favor. (Not that you can't make it work either way. I just find it a little more effective to do this work in person.) Then, once you reach the outline phase, you can pretty much work in separate locations the rest of the way, again passing documents back and forth until you're satisfied with them.

When writing the actual script, I've found that the best way to ensure that each of your voices is being fairly represented is to write no more than a scene or two before you pass it back to your partner. You'll also need to establish some ground rules at this point, governing how extensively each of you can rewrite the other. Here's an arrangement that works particularly well:

As long as each writer remains consistent with the outline, all rewriting is fair. However, if either writer wants to do something that represents a significant departure from what has already been mutually agreed upon, then a conversation needs to take place before any blood can be drawn.

As you can imagine, this process can definitely get a little trying at times. Each partner can have a very different take on the nuances of how each character behaves, how each character sounds, and how a particular scene should go (even when you've agreed upon its placement and its content).

Regardless of the arrangement, one thing remains absolutely true:

You've got to be willing to compromise when you work with a writing partner.

You also have to be able to exercise a great deal of tolerance and patience—which means completely buying into *we* at the expense of *me*.

SURVIVAL GUIDE SUMMARY

10. Writing Partners

Things to Remember:

- Being in a writing partnership is like being in a marriage. It's an intimate relationship that needs to be based on trust, mutual respect, and commitment.

- The partner process takes time to evolve. You have to work at it.

- It's usually best to be in the same room with one another through the brainstorming, concept, and structuring phases.

- Once you begin outlining, it's easier to be in separate spaces, passing documents back and forth.

- Remain passionate about your ideas, but always be willing to compromise with your partner.

Questions to Ask Yourself:

- Are you willing to give up creative ownership of the work and be a 50-50 partner in it?

- Are you prepared to negotiate every creative decision with your partner if necessary?

- Are you willing to sacrifice your own voice as a writer for the sake of the voice that emerges as a product of the partnership?

- What creative ground rules have you set for your process? Under what circumstances is it okay to rewrite your partner and vice versa?

- Are you dividing the workload equally? Try not to cross the 50-yard line too often.

11. Pitching Stories

Pitching a story really isn't all that different from pitching any other kind of product. Sure, it's a creative idea you're talking about, so it's a lot more glamorous than pitching a vacuum cleaner or a bottle of shampoo, but at the end of the day it's still a *sales pitch* and you, as the writer, are the *salesman*—which, frankly, has always made me a bit uncomfortable.

"I'm not a salesman, damn it! I'm a writer!" I want to scream to the heavens every time I have to work on a pitch (and sometimes do). But like it or not, pitching is part of the job. At some point, it's not enough to just lock yourself up in a dark room and crank out pages. You have to be able to verbally express your ideas to people, to give them confidence that you *can* go off and write that great script. So you might as well find a way to get good at this little dog-and-pony show or, at the very least, figure out an impressive way to fake it. (Just kidding. There is no way to fake it, really. So you *better* get good at it!)

Pitch Your Personality

When you walk into that room to pitch a story, the most important thing you're selling is yourself. Like any other business meeting or job interview, your would-be buyers/employers are looking for talented people with exciting ideas, but first and foremost they're looking for a person that they can work with, a person that they don't mind talking to on the phone a couple times a day or whose name doesn't make them shudder every time it appears in their e-mail. The only way to be that person is to be authentic. In other words:

You have to pitch in a way that's consistent with your personality.

Here's a perfect example. I have two very successful writer friends, one in film and the other in television. The film guy is very soft-spoken. He pitches like a fisherman with a secret. He starts off very quietly, then slowly reels his audience in as he carefully unspools his story, giving them one bite-size piece of information after the other, until he finally reveals all. The TV guy is the complete opposite. He pitches like a three-ring circus rolling into town: big, gregarious, colorful, and bursting at the seams with enthusiasm. Not that he's blustery and loud. He's not. It's just a very energetic, get-your-popcorn-ready type of approach. Both styles are extremely effective, but not necessarily because they're technically proficient (which they are). They're effective because they're authentic and they're consistent with each writer's personality.

My personality is much closer to my TV pal's. I get very animated when I'm passionate about something, and nothing gets me more amped up than talking about a story, so I pretty much allow that excitement to come through when I pitch. Again, it's all about being comfortable in your own skin. Beyond that, the key is to be really well prepared and have a good, solid framework through which you can both deliver the content and focus your energy, regardless of your style or approach.

A Pitch Is a Performance

Pitching is very much like acting. It's a performance, a little piece of theater in which the character that you're playing is *you*. So when I say you need to be well prepared and have a framework, what I really mean is you need to know what you're going to say, and like an actor, you need to rehearse and deliver your lines as if they're coming out of your mouth for the very first time.

Does this mean you should write yourself an actual script just for the pitch? If you feel it will help you, absolutely. It all depends on what you're comfortable with and also, to some degree, the specifics of the particular project.

I've written myself pitch scripts at times, but generally I tend to prefer to write it in my head as I talk it through to myself, over and over, and commit it to memory. I find that I'm a little less attached to the specific words when I do it that way, and a little more focused on the beats of the story and the big ideas. I also feel that this technique makes it a bit easier to pick up where I left off after being interrupted, which will happen in almost every pitch meeting.

Either way, whether you write yourself a script or just write it in your head, you have to know the material backward and forward.

Pitching with Partners

Pitching with a partner (or multiple partners) allows you to enjoy many of the same advantages that writing with a partner does, the greatest of which is that you don't have to carry the whole load by yourself. Even if you're a great pitchman, it's always nice to have that other person in the room to play off of. Two or more voices are also much easier on the ear of the listener than one because of the natural variety in tone and inflection that's created. The trick is to alternate speaking at palatable intervals, which means you really have to be on the same page and know who is going to say what and when. In other words:

You have to be working from the same script.

Fortunately, most of the people that I've developed projects with over the years have shared this approach to partner pitching, but there was one occasion when it was definitely put to the test.

Not too long ago I was pitching an interactive project in which I had two partners. The project also involved demonstrating some innovative technology designed for live performances, so it wasn't exactly like pitching a television show or a movie, but the same principles apply. We needed to sell our personalities in the room, we needed to tell an engaging story, and above all, we needed to work together with precision and give a good performance. The problem was that one of my partners wasn't too keen on rehearsing. Not that he was lazy or didn't care. In fact, he was very committed. He just didn't have that much experience pitching and felt that rehearsing would cause us to lose our freshness. He didn't quite get the concept of being a well-rehearsed actor, and insisted on just winging it. So the third guy and I rehearsed our parts as best we could without him. Sure enough, when we got into the room, guess which one of us got flustered and stumbled over his words?

The last thing you want to happen in a pitch meeting is to look unsure of yourself. Even if you actually know the material cold and just have a momentary lapse, the instant that happens it puts a seed of doubt in the buyer's mind about whether or not you can do the job. So why take that chance? Why not do everything in your power ahead of time to prevent that from happening?

One bad experience was all it took to make my interactive pal a believer. The next time out, he was much more amenable to rehearsing his part and, not surprisingly, came off much more confident in the meeting.

Be Open and Flexible

I don't want to be a buzz killer here, but it wouldn't be very forthright of me if I didn't tell you that the majority of your pitches will probably not result in a happy ending. It's a sobering fact, I know, especially given how much of a writer's heart and soul goes into telling a good story, but as any salesman will tell you, pitching is a numbers game. You have to get a lot of people to say "no" before someone says "yes."

The thing about pitching in the entertainment business that makes this fact even more maddening is that the decision to buy or not is highly subjective and unpredictable. There are so many factors beyond just the merits of what you're offering that go into it: for example, what the company already has in development, if there's a budget to buy your pitch, what is currently working in the marketplace, etc. And sometimes when you do get that "yes," it doesn't come exactly the way you expected. That's why it's so important to be open and flexible, and ready for anything that happens in the room that might even *lead* to a yes.

Here's another story for you that illustrates this point. After I had written an episode of a television show called *The Invisible Man*, the producers were so happy with the job I'd done for them they asked me to come back in and pitch another one. This obviously didn't guarantee me another sale, but naturally I was very excited and immediately shifted my brain into overdrive to come up with that next great pitch.

Now you remember my buddy, the acupuncturist, who lets me use his office? Here's a case where not only was the environment a wonderful creative cocoon that allowed me to do my best work, it also gave me the perfect idea.

In the show the main character, Darien Fawkes, has a synthetic gland implanted in his brain by a secret government agency. The gland allows Darien to turn invisible but it's not without its glitches, as he can't always control his invisibility. My idea was that, during a mission, Darien wrenches his back and subsequently goes for acupuncture in a desperate attempt to both heal himself and alleviate the pain. But when the acupuncturist puts the needles in him, she inadvertently stimulates the gland and discovers that *she* can control it—which inevitably leads to no good.

As always, I put as much work into the story as time would allow, diligently prepared, and then went in and pitched my heart out. From the get-go all the writers in the room responded to the idea, but when I was done the executive producer said: "All right, forget everything he said after the word 'acupuncturist,' and let's see if there's actually a story here that we can use."

At that point it would have been very easy for me to let my bruised ego do the talking, to just keep trying to convince them the material I'd prepared was in fact worthy of another episode. A younger version of me may very well have done that. Actually, younger versions of me *did* do that, which is why this time I made sure I'd learned from my previous mistakes. This time I played it smart. I knew I had a "yes." It may not have been the "yes" I'd wanted or expected, but it was definitely a "yes." All I had to do to close the deal was know when to shut up.

To make the sale I'd have to settle for selling the *idea* and not the exact story I'd pitched. So, rather than being defensive and possibly end up *talking them out of saying* "yes," wasn't it better to let my pitch basically be the first draft and let the brainstorm that was now occurring in the meeting be the first revision?

This calculation turned out to be right on the money. The pitch was successful. I got the job. Not only that, they bought the next two episodes I pitched them. Why? Because I pitched my personality, I was always well prepared, *and* I was open and flexible enough to let that "yes" take whatever form it was going to take.

Know Your Audience

Another very important part of pitching involves not just pitching your personality, but also understanding the personality of the person you're pitching to. Obviously, if you've never met the person before, there's no way of knowing what they're like, but if you've had the chance to get to know them even a little bit, then you owe it to yourself to specifically tailor your pitch to the aspects you know they will respond to (to whatever extent that's possible).

Recently I was working on a project at Walt Disney Imagineering, which is the part of Disney that builds the theme parks, and found myself pitching to an executive I'd pitched to several times before. Now, because WDI has such a tried-and-true creative process and such a rich tradition, you typically follow a certain protocol when you pitch there, using a style of storytelling that is very unique to what they do.

In this case, however, I didn't feel confident the traditional approach would work. Why? Because this particular executive is extremely adept at figuring out what you're going to say ahead of time and, once he does, tends to cut you off before you've had a chance to fully explain it. This doesn't mean he's no longer interested in your concept. It's just that in the blink of an eye, he's two steps ahead of you, which inevitably leaves you scrambling to get out from behind the eight ball.

I knew the standard dog-and-pony show wasn't going to work this time, so instead, I decided to bring in three people who were supporting me on the project and use *them* to tell my story. Rather than formally pitching, I kept the whole thing conversational, sort of backing into each part of the pitch by saying something like: "John and I were discussing the first part of the experience, and his idea, which I really liked, was to do X, Y, and Z." We'd then talk about that aspect of the project for a while, and then I'd somewhat stealthily move on to the next part of the pitch by steering the discussion in the direction of another one of my supporting players.

The resulting conversation was not only very enlightening, but also very effective, as I kept this very smart executive engaged in the story throughout the entire meeting, and most importantly, convinced him to provide funding for another round of development on the project.

SURVIVAL GUIDE SUMMARY

11. Pitching Stories

Things to Remember:

- Pitching is a necessary evil. You must be able to express your ideas verbally as well as on paper in order to give potential employers confidence that you can do the job.

- The most important thing you're selling when pitching a story is yourself. So pitch your personality.

- A pitch is a performance in which you are both the actor and the main character.

- Memorize your pitch, then perform it as though you're saying the words for the first time, just like a good actor.

- Hone your pitch so you use as few words as possible. Try to make it no longer than 10 to 15 minutes.

- When pitching with a partner, figure out ahead of time exactly who is going to say what and when.

- Be open and flexible. Anything can happen once you get in the room.

Questions to Ask Yourself:

- What's your natural storytelling style? Are you big and gregarious? Quiet and soft-spoken?

- How do you tell stories to your friends or family members in everyday life? Develop an approach that is similar.

- Is there a hook to your pitch you can use to start it off right? A personal anecdote, for example, or a metaphor that frames the theme of your story and sets the tone for the rest of the pitch?

- Which parts of your story can be edited out in your verbal presentation? Look hard at each beat as you rehearse and only include what's absolutely necessary.

- Who are you pitching to? Have you pitched to them before? Tailor your pitch to receive the most favorable response possible.

12. Writing for Hire

Up until now, most of what we've been discussing is writing original material on spec. "Writing for hire" or "writing on assignment" is when you either get paid to write someone else's story or when you pitch an idea and the buyer pays you to write it (as in the TV example in the previous chapter).

Writing on spec is your lifeblood as a writer, not just because you're creating intellectual property that has inherent value, but even more importantly because you're creating writing samples that can help you get work for hire—which is far more likely to happen than selling a spec script.

If this comes as news to you, do a little survey of the movies playing down at your local multiplex or on the cable box in your living room. You'll find that most of them are not based on original screenplays. Most are based on material from other mediums: novels, comic books, myths and fairytales, old television shows, or they're remakes or sequels of other movies. If you dig a little deeper, you'll also find that many of the movies that *were* based on original scripts were actually developed after the ideas were either pitched or assigned to a writer (not written on spec).

Likewise, in television, almost all episode ideas are pitched before they're written, either by writers working on a show's writing staff or by freelancers like me on *The Invisible Man*. Even pilot episodes, which form the bedrock of a series and must be created entirely from scratch (except when they too are based on other material) are mostly sold as pitches first, with a few exceptions.

In the interactive world, where I've spent a healthy chunk of my career, virtually all development is internal, particularly at video game companies. They simply don't take pitches from the outside. All creative ideas are generated from within, so the only way to write a narrative script for a video game (if you're not an employee of the company) *is* to be a writer for hire.

So what does all this mean? For one thing it means when you work for hire, once again, there is no draft for you. Just like when you write with a partner, it's a *we* thing, not a *me* thing from the moment you sign on. It also means that you have to be mentally prepared for the various work requirements, conditions, and expectations that come along with each project. You won't have the luxury of exclusively operating in that wonderful creative cocoon of your own mind like you do when you work on spec. You will, however, still have the one invaluable thing you will always need to pull off the job—your *process*.

Every experience will present you with new and unique challenges, so the more you hone that process, the more tools and techniques you develop for yourself, the better equipped you will be to handle each and every assignment.

The Note Giver Is Always Right

I'm sure you've heard the old business adage: "The customer is always right." As a writer for hire you've got to operate under this same principle. You're the businessman, the shopkeeper selling the goods and the customer is your note giver.

I've had some great experiences throughout my writing life, working in many different mediums. I've made a lot of wonderful friends, lifelong friends in some cases, and have worked for many producers, directors, creative directors, and executives for whom I have the utmost respect. But I'm not going to mince words here. It's not always easy. In fact, most of the time there is at least some level of tension involved in this relationship. How can there not be if the note giver is *always* right?

Not that you don't fully engage with them, doing everything in your power to shape the notes and create the best product you possibly can every time out. It's just that when push comes to shove, they're paying you for your services, so it's *their project*, not yours—which means that you also have to be incredibly tolerant when they are unclear, unexpectedly change their mind, or flat out tell you they're not satisfied with your work.

Sometimes tension exists in the relationship simply because the note giver isn't comfortable with the job. After all, not everyone is built to deal with writers and the painstaking process of developing ideas and creating written material (not even some writers). Sometimes there are other things in the mix that cause problems, none of which has anything to do with you: production deadlines, personal issues, intra-office politics, etc.

Other times it has *everything* to do with you. Maybe you're not cast right for the project. Maybe you just missed the mark on this one. It happens. Nobody's perfect.

And then sometimes…well, unfortunately sometimes you end up working for people who are just downright nasty about the whole thing and out to make your life miserable.

Trust me, no writer worth their salt has ever been able to fully escape this fate. I've been on the receiving end of some pretty ugly behavior over the years, on the part of both individuals and companies that have hired (and sometimes fired) me, none of which I care to recount, much less remember. All I can tell you is that you've got to develop a thick skin when it comes to this, shall we say, darker side of the profession.

There *will* be times when you feel that you've been treated unfairly. That's just part of the deal, another unpleasant fact that you've got to accept, courtesy of your writer gene. The important thing to remember is:

It's the integrity of the work that matters most, even in the worst of situations.

It's the dedication to your craft, the commitment to yourself as a writer, and the fidelity to your process that will keep you going through these rocky moments.

Don't Be a Writing Student—Be a Writer for Hire

As I mentioned earlier, one of the things that surprised me most about film school was the rather stunning revelation that there was no *secret sauce* to being a good writer. Though there are definitely much better writing programs and much better teachers out there today than there were back when I first got off the bus in L.A., I still believe that this is fundamentally true. Creative writing of any kind is so cerebral that even when you're actively taking classes, the most impactful learning happens when you're *actually writing*, not when you're in class.

One thing you can and should do to take full advantage of that classroom experience, however, is develop the skills that you'll need to be successful with the note givers you'll encounter after you graduate. So if you're a writing student, whether you're in college, graduate school, or some other specialized writing program, my advice is that you approach your coursework as if it were a job. In other words:

Don't be a writing student. Be a writer for hire.

While you will probably be developing original stories in your classes, the teacher and the other writers will also be influencing your work from very early on in the process. This means that, once again, this is a case where you don't have the luxury of keeping the story to yourself for weeks and months and years. Again, there's no draft for you because you are *required* to discuss your ideas with the group and then use their feedback to develop them. Sounds a lot more like writing for hire than it does writing on spec, doesn't it?

Now, I realize you're not getting paid for this work. On the contrary, you're *paying them* for the opportunity to acquire essential knowledge, but the forum is not all that different from the one you'll experience when you get hired to write something in the real world. There's a primary note giver, and then there are others who will also be contributing ideas you'll have to consider. So instead of being insulted by inane comments, or arguing with your teacher or your peers, or being frustrated by the fact that no one is "getting it," why not work on some of the skills that you know you'll definitely need to have in your back pocket later on?

In case some of this stuff has already slipped your mind, here's a little review: First, try and approach the project like it's *theirs*, not yours. Get yourself into an open frame of mind each and every time you walk into class. Understand that the story never stops being told, and that the note giver is always right. Then, focus on your note-receiving skills, see how nimbly you can use the conversation about your work to shape it into the story that *you* envision. Above all, show the people in the room that you value their opinions and make them your allies.

If you can find a way to step into these writer-for-hire shoes throughout the course of your next writing class, my guess is you're pretty likely to get your money's worth.

Always Have a Project in the Back of the Shop

Have you ever gone to some local mom-and-pop type store, caught a glimpse into the back of the shop, and seen something you didn't quite expect? Maybe mom's got this amazing wedding dress she's designing back there, or pop has some kind of mad scientist chemistry set that he's using to invent a new kind of super glue. These are their passion projects, the things they work on a few hours a night after everyone else goes home.

As a writer working for hire, you've got to have this same mentality. No matter how successful you are, you can never get complacent.

You always need to have a passion project going on in the back of the shop.

Why is this important? Because spending the majority of your time and energy working on something that isn't one hundred percent yours will eventually take a toll on you, as will the constant burden of receiving and executing the associated notes. Having a project in the back of the shop, a project where there *is* a draft just for you, will feed your soul in a way that no work for hire ever can, even if it's just a sweet little snack for you to enjoy a couple times a week. At the same time, this work will also help you continue to develop your own voice, which like any other muscle will begin to atrophy in the absence of exercise.

Finally, on a more practical note, this extra effort will not only result in the creation of another piece of original material you can potentially sell, it will also give you a fresh new writing sample, and as any working writer will tell you, you can never have enough samples.

SURVIVAL GUIDE SUMMARY

12. Writing for Hire

Things to Remember:

- You need great writing samples in order to get work for hire, which means writing on spec is essential.

- When you work as a writer for hire there is no draft for you. It's a *we* thing, not a *me* thing, from the very beginning.

- Your process is more important than ever when writing for hire. It's the one thing you can always fall back on to get you through the rocky moments.

- When you work as a writer for hire, the note giver is always right.

- As a writer, there will always be some degree of tension involved in the relationship between you and your employer. It's okay. Just accept it.

- If you're taking a writing class, approach the work as if it's a job. Don't be a writing student, be a writer for hire.

- Always have a passion project going on in the back of the shop. It will feed your soul.

Questions to Ask Yourself:

- What can you do to make the working relationship with your employer as productive as possible?

- Which are the most important battles to fight with respect to the work? Choose wisely. You can't win them all.

- How can you use your creative talent to solve any issue that arises between you and your employer, writing-related or otherwise?

- Which is better for the project (and for your career)—to be effective or to be right?

- If you're a writing student, what are the ways in which you can effectively turn your class into a work for hire? What do you want to get from your teacher? From your peers? Write down some goals.

- How can you shape the notes you get in class into something that is consistent with your vision?

13. Art vs. Commerce

Many years ago, my wife and I were in Paris and visited the Musée d'Orsay, where we were lucky enough to catch an extraordinary Vincent van Gogh exhibit that had a very profound effect on me. It was a modest collection, only about fifteen or twenty paintings located in a very small room, so it wasn't so much the volume of the work that made such an impression. It was the fact that they were all self-portraits.

I'm sure that putting the exhibit in a somewhat claustrophobic room was a very intentional decision on the part of the curator. You couldn't help but feel an unbelievable rush of emotion the moment you walked in there. There he was, arguably one of the greatest artists who ever lived, staring at you from every direction, the sorrow in his eyes, the pain he suffered throughout his life so palpable. And to think that this incredibly gifted man went to his grave without ever having the satisfaction of knowing how immensely valuable his work would soon become. It's hard to imagine a greater injustice.

I don't bring this up to be a buzz killer again, but to simply illustrate the point that:

Financial success is one thing and artistic success is entirely another.

Van Gogh was clearly a brilliant painter, but the fact that he never achieved financial success in his lifetime obviously doesn't diminish his artistic achievements in any way. The two are not joined at the hip. I think the same could be said of writers and writing. We've all heard the stories of the great Hollywood scripts that languished for years and years before someone finally championed them and made them into classic films, or the great authors who experienced financial hardship before achieving both critical acclaim *and* financial success. Believe it or not, for every Mario Puzo or J. K. Rowling that's been lucky enough to break into the public consciousness, there are thousands, if not tens of thousands, of other writers who may not be rich and famous but whose work is truly exceptional, as well as worthy of being enjoyed by far more people than will ever have the pleasure of being exposed to it.

Furthermore, financial success is completely objective. You can touch financial success. You can literally count it and define it in terms of dollars and cents. It's different for each individual of course, but it's still the result of a concrete, mathematical formula. For some writers, it may simply mean getting paid any amount of money to write (i.e., financial success = receiving anything greater than zero for writing), while other writers may not consider themselves financially successful unless they make at least six figures a year from writing. Still, any way you slice it, financial success is a clear, tangible thing. Writing success, on the other hand, is entirely subjective. It's something that no one can touch or count.

So all other things being equal, including talent level, why are some writers more financially successful than others?

This question has a two-part answer. First, achieving financial success isn't really all that different for writers than it is for any given population of people in any other profession. There are just things some people do well that eventually results in more money in their wallets —the way they present themselves; the way they interact with their colleagues, their clients, and their associates; the way they're able to gather a supporting cast around them. This is all stuff you can learn. Sure, some of it's instinctual, but for the most part it's all about being good at the *business* of being a writer.

Second, as any successful businessman will tell you, sometimes you just have to be lucky. This, obviously, is *not* something you can learn. You have to be at the right place at the right time —and in the case of writers, with a well-executed idea.

Which brings us back to writing success.

Writing Success = Writer Gene + Process

I always get a kick out of hearing people say that they wrote a feature-length screenplay in six days. I don't know why it's always six days and not five or seven, but for some reason it is. When people do this, they want you to think either (A) they're some kind of genius, or (B) that they were so blessed by this moment of divine inspiration, the thing just came bursting fully grown out of their brain, like Athena from the head of Zeus.

The truth is that no one can write a screenplay in six days, not a good one anyway, and certainly not a great one. The only way to write anything great is to have both the talent to write it and the drive to spend as much time as it takes to make it the very best it can be. In other words, the formula for writing success is:

Writing Success = Writer Gene + Process

Achieving writing success is a marathon, not a sprint. It's about continuing to hone your process so that each successive piece of work over the course of your writing life grows and improves over the last one. It's about going deeper into all the aspects of the craft. It's about developing your command of the language. It's about being more efficient, learning from your mistakes, and becoming an expert in each and every medium that you choose to write in.

Most importantly, writing success is something that can only be measured by your own internal yardstick. Only you know what you're capable of. Only you know how far you can push yourself, how many ideas you can come up with, how well you can execute them, and how many times you can rewrite that script over and over and over again. Writing success only happens when you can look yourself in the mirror and honestly say that you've done everything in your power to make a story work, that you've tuned that radio in and brought that signal through as clearly and completely as you possibly can.

That's not to say that achieving writing success is totally divorced from getting the positive feedback of others. Let's be honest, it would be pretty naïve (not to mention, a little delusional) to claim that you've written a successful story if you haven't received at least some modicum of external validation. But I think it's also fair to say that the feedback you receive is ultimately only one factor among many that determines whether or not you feel you've fully realized any given piece of work. The real test is how well you stack up to that internal yardstick, whether or not you've reached the highest of bars you've set for yourself and satisfied the fairest, wisest, and most discerning of critics—*you*.

When you've done that, I believe you've achieved success as a writer. And when you can do it consistently, I believe financial success will follow.

SURVIVAL GUIDE SUMMARY

13. Art vs. Commerce

Things to Remember:

- Financial success and writing success are not joined at the hip.

- You can learn the business of being a writer. But you also have to be lucky to be financially successful.

- The best way to get lucky is to be ready when luck comes your way—which means having a great script in your pocket.

- Writing success = writer gene + process. It's a marathon, not a sprint.

- Only you know when you have achieved writing success.

Questions to Ask Yourself:

- What is the definition of financial success for you as a writer? Write it down.

- Have you looked at your overall writing process and identified places where you need to improve?

- What can you do differently on your next project, process-wise, that might help you overcome some of the deficiencies in your last one?

- Have you rewritten the story you're currently working on as much as you possibly can? Do you know in your heart that it is as good as you can make it?

14. The Write Community

When I started writing this survival guide, I have to admit, I hadn't really given much thought to how much my experience at The American Film Institute has shaped my thinking as a writer, and I certainly didn't think I would be talking about it as much as I have. But as I reflect on it now, I realize it really did have a tremendous impact. The reason for that is simple. From the very first moment I stepped onto that campus, I felt I had finally found "my people." I had finally become part of a community where everyone was passionate about telling stories, and where the words that made up those stories mattered. For the first time in my life, I had finally gotten into a room with a bunch of other writers.

Looking back on those days it seems as if my classmates and I were living in a timeless bubble. The long afternoons we spent sitting at that little sushi joint on the corner of Franklin and Vermont, arguing endlessly about theme and structure and characters. The hours and hours we spent watching films. The countless seminars we were so privileged to attend with the world's greatest filmmakers. It was total and complete immersion into *writer land*, an unforgettable journey, free of all the other encumbrances of life.

While that experience could obviously never be duplicated, it did convince me of one very important thing:

To whatever extent it's possible, you should make every effort to surround yourself with a community of writers, throughout every stage of your career.

Bonding with Your Writer Brethren

Why is this such a big deal? Why do writers need other writers? Because when you spend the majority of your time living in the vast reaches of that infinite universe we call the human mind, every once in a while you just need someone to talk to. You know, an *actual person* who can *actually* sit down across from you and look you in the eye, as opposed to yet another figment of your imagination. But not just anybody will fit that bill. You need someone who truly knows what you're going through day in and day out, someone who understands the solitude firsthand, who shares your passion, and who, like you, just may be crazy enough to spend their entire life pursuing it. These kinds of conversations between writers, whether they happen in passing or over a two-hour lunch, are so powerful and so vital to our collective psyche. It's that unspoken solidarity, that exchange of energy and encouragement, that so often provides just the spark we need to press on.

On a more practical level, bonding with your writer brethren also allows you to share strategies and learn about the different techniques they may use. As your process continues to evolve, you will inevitably find yourself experimenting with these various approaches you hear about. They may not always work for you, but at the very least they will inform you creatively and contribute to your overall knowledge of the craft.

Here's an interesting example. I have a friend who likes to experiment with the validity of his story concepts by writing test scenes. In other words, when he stumbles onto an idea he thinks is good, he immediately dives in and writes the one scene that is clearest in his mind, just to see if it pops on the page as much as it did in his head. Usually it's a scene near the end of the story, a big climactic moment that he's envisioning. His thinking is that if he can make the test scene work (even if he completely rewrites it later), then he'll have an aiming point that will give him the drive and momentum needed to start writing the story from the beginning.

I found this fascinating, because while this approach is absolutely 180 degrees from my process, it's also very similar to how I often write extensive notes about scenes that occur later in my story while I'm outlining. The difference is that I still start at the highest level of the concept and work my way down to the details. In his case, he's actually writing an entire fleshed-out scene before he's even done a stitch of research or made a single note about his idea.

The thing that has always struck me about this particular writer friend of mine is the ease with which he blindly follows his instincts. The openness that he allows himself in his process, the fearless, optimistic way that he experiments with ideas is just tremendous. And while the form it takes for him—actually writing the scene with no context—is not something that would work for me, the concept behind it, the exploratory element, is certainly a very important aspect of my process as well.

Cultivating Community

Besides all the shop talk, there are so many other ways that simply connecting with other writers can pay valuable dividends. It exposes you to resources, like interesting classes, books, and seminars to help educate yourself. It helps you find great environments to work in. For example, I heard about The Writers Junction, the place where I go to write almost every day now, through a writer friend of mine.

Your extended writer community is also how you will find good note givers (writers and non-writers alike), producers and directors to collaborate with, and agents and managers who could potentially represent you. You might even find a great writing partner to work with if you're engaged with a community of writers.

By far the greatest benefit to cultivating this community around you is that it allows you to talk about your stories on a level only other writers can appreciate, and in a way that reveals who you truly are. When you share your ideas with other writers you are saying to them: "Check this out. This is what turns me on as an artist!" And the mere act of doing so proves your worth. It's how you plant your flag as someone who belongs in this community and inspires others to do the same. That kind of energy and vitality is contagious and can easily spread like wildfire—which is exactly what we all need in order to become better storytellers.

Writing Groups

One of the best ways to cultivate a writer community around you is to form or join a writing group. What you do with this group is get together on a regular basis to give each other notes and help improve each other's work. In other words, you basically create your own writing class, except that there is no teacher and no institution behind it. Typically groups like this consist of about five to ten writers, all of whom must be serious enough about their careers to commit not just to the meetings, but to all the reading each member must do in order for the group to be valuable. As I explained in Chapter 7, giving good notes takes a considerable amount of work, and if you're going to have any hope of doing it well, you have to be willing to roll up your sleeves and get your hands dirty right alongside the fellow writer(s) you're trying to help.

It's also important for all the writers in the group to be somewhat compatible in terms of talent level, craft, and professional experience. This is easier said than done, particularly when it comes to getting the right mix of personalities. If you're lucky enough to assemble a committed bunch of people and create a productive, healthy dynamic, it can be a truly wonderful and empowering experience. The secret to creating that special chemistry is to find quality writers who are also willing to become quality note givers, and who understand that by investing their time and energy in others, they're also investing in themselves.

(To learn more about the online community for writers I'm currently developing please visit www.thewritergene.com.)

SURVIVAL GUIDE SUMMARY

14. The Write Community

Things to Remember:

- To whatever extent possible, make every effort to surround yourself with a community of other writers throughout every stage of your career.

- Writers need other writers not just for moral support, but also for the exchange of energy and ideas.

- Your community of writers is your umbilical cord to numerous resources, potential collaborators, and representatives.

- Being part of a community of writers helps you express who you are as an artist.

- One of the best ways to cultivate a community of writers is to start or join a writing group.

Questions to Ask Yourself:

- Do you know any writers who are as serious about writing as you are? Who are they? Make a list.

- Have you ever sat down and had an in-depth conversation about process with these writers? How are your processes different?

- Is there anything these other writers do that you might experiment with? Anything useful that you think you might be able to incorporate into your process?

- What aspects of your process can you share with them?

- Do you know five to ten other writers who might make a good writing group? Do you know of any existing writing groups that you might be able to join?

15. Live to Write Another Day

As I discussed in the previous chapter, among the many things I truly cherish about being a writer are the bonds of friendship and camaraderie I've forged over the years with other writers. On a practical level, these bonds are an important way to learn and grow, as even the most casual conversation with a writer friend can spark a new idea or shed some light on a frustrating problem. On another level, they're like comfort food, a reminder that we're not alone, that we have brethren out there toiling in the trenches. On an even deeper level, I believe these bonds are the result of a much more powerful impulse, that as creative storytellers we are bound together by a higher purpose, a calling to be the cultural record keepers of our generation.

Now that you've gotten to know me a little bit, I'm sure you understand how passionate I am about this calling, that I really do see the writing life as something you have no choice but to pursue if you have the writer gene, and that it's an epic struggle in which you must be a warrior of the highest order, the hero of your own story.

You owe it to yourself to be that hero, to honor that calling each and every day, regardless of your circumstances, regardless of your previous successes or failures, regardless of whether the journey takes you into calm seas or into the most violent of storms.

You may not share all my feelings about writing or see eye to eye with me on everything in this survival guide, but if nothing else, I hope I have at least given you a little inspiration and created yet another bond within our sacred tribe. You have my utmost respect for being a writer, for having the fortitude to bear your soul on the page day after day, for taking the chance that you may never be able to make that idea work—or that even when you do, that story may never quite get its fair day in court with the many gatekeepers who never seem to miss an opportunity to deny you the key to the city.

I know how difficult it is to do what you're trying to do, how much of yourself it requires, how agonizing it is when all that effort fails to bear any fruit, either artistically or financially. And, boy, do I know how hard it is to pick yourself up off the canvas for the umpteenth time, to draw your sword and take another swing at that monstrous creature…again and again and again.

All I can say is:

Don't stop swinging! Don't stop taking those chances, because it's out of all that vulnerability, out of all that risk taking, that the most profound work inevitably emerges.

No great script was ever written by a writer playing it safe. So whatever you do, never be afraid to sail into those uncharted waters. Never be afraid to go down with the ship. There's not a writer on this earth who hasn't come up short on what they once thought was the most brilliant idea, so you won't be the first and you certainly won't be the last. It's on the rubble of those discarded pages that the foundation of your career will ultimately be built, and not one of your successes will come without the many failings that came before it. Not that success is ever guaranteed, but if you have the courage to go on this journey in the first place, then I believe you'll have the courage to see it through, and there will never be a doubt in your mind as to whether or not you were up to the challenge.

Just know that your voice is worthy of being heard, that the fight to make it heard is never in vain, and that if you stay true to that voice, if you commit to developing your skills and continue to hone and love your process, if you always remember that the story is out there in its purest and most perfect form, that it exists separately from you, and that you are both its mother and its guardian, your work will always be consistent and unique to who you are.

Most importantly, if you can learn how to share your story with the common culture, to let it be influenced but not misguided, to change and revise it in ways that not only deepen its characters and shore up its structure, but also magnify its core message, then there are no limits to the writer you can become.

All you have to do is hang in there a little longer, tune that story in a little clearer, and live to write another day.

SURVIVAL GUIDE SUMMARY

15. Live to Write Another Day

Things to Remember:

- As creative storytellers, we are the cultural record keepers of our generation.

- Be the hero of your own story. Never give up!

- Don't be afraid to fail. No great story was ever written by a writer playing it safe.

- Your voice is worthy of being heard, and the fight to make it heard is never in vain.

COMPLETE SURVIVAL GUIDE

1. The Writer Gene

Things to Remember:

- If you're a person who is driven to tell stories with words, then you have the writer gene.

- Guess what—you're not alone.

2. The Art of Procrastination

Things to Remember:

- Procrastination is part of the creative process.

- Procrastination is only bad if you create anxiety about procrastinating. Don't beat yourself up about it. Use it.

- You are both a passive and active channel of information when you write.

Questions to Ask Yourself:

- What procrastination activities contribute to your process? Make a list.

- What procrastination activities are destructive to your process? Make a list.

- How much procrastination time will you allow yourself when you sit down to write? Be specific.

3. The Write Environment

Things to Remember:

- To be productive on a regular basis, find environments that are consistently available to you.

- Make sure these environments have limited distractions and temptations. All you really need is a desk, a chair, and a power outlet.

- If an environment works for you, keep using it! It won't take long for you to associate it with successful writing, which will help build your confidence.

- A change of scenery sometimes helps the creative flow.

Questions to Ask Yourself:

- Which parts of your process can you do in a noisier environment, and which require absolute quietude? Make a list.

- Of the different environments available to you, which can you work in on a consistent basis? Can you make each of them a reliable writing silo?

- What are the available hours of each of your writing silos? Make a list.

- How many hours on any given day do you need to spend in each silo to be productive? Plan it out ahead of time.

- Is there a place near you where other writers write? It's always good to be around other writers.

4. Writer's Bl%#k

Things to Remember:

- Writer's bl%#k is a myth. Every creative problem has a creative solution.

- All writers experience crisis moments.

- Knowing that the solution to the crisis exists is half the battle.

- The other half of the battle is having a process that you can rely on.

- Breathe.

Questions to Ask Yourself:

- Have you run into this problem before? Most of the time the answer is "yes." How did you solve it last time?

- If you haven't run into this specific problem before, how is it similar to other problems you've encountered?

- How long did it take you to solve your last crisis? Be conscious of this time factor. There's usually a pattern.

- What is the strongest aspect of your core concept? Are you still speaking to it or have you strayed? Don't panic. Just take some time to re-examine the big picture.

- Is there a specific place earlier in your story (preceding the crisis point) that is not quite as solid as you thought? Take a good look. This is probably the root of your problem.

- Are you remembering to breathe?

5. Tuning In the Radio

Things to Remember:

- All original stories exist in a perfect state as thought forms that are separate from you. Listen and tune them in like a radio signal.

- Begin with research. This is the soundest foundation you can set for your process.

- By taking the time to build a foundation of research, crisis moments are less likely to occur.

- Be a passive channel of information while you research, taking lots of notes without editing yourself. Let the ideas flow without judgment.

- Transcribe your notes at the end of your research period. Creating this Notes Document allows you to kick off your project without ever having to stare at a blank page.

- Create a Concept Document from your Notes Document. Avoid the temptation to rush into the outline or the first draft.

- Structure your story by writing the scenes on index cards or a whiteboard so you can view them as separate moments, rearranging them as necessary.

- Begin your outline by writing down all the scenes you have so far. Get all your ideas on the table without worrying about getting the story right. Your process will naturally fill in the blanks.

- Describe the scenes in your outline without actually writing them. Your outline is a road map, not the final product.

- Note deeper character motivations and other important story points in your outline. The deeper you dig, the more material you will have to work with.

- Once you've figured out most of your story structure, write all the scenes down on one or two pages of a legal pad, using one line for each scene, then skim the story to see if it flows.

Questions to Ask Yourself:

- What is the backdrop of your story and how can you learn more about it?

- Which websites will tell you more about your story's larger world and help you develop important details about your characters? Identify and print relevant materials. Bookmark the sites for future reference.

- Which books are available that will educate you about your story's world and its characters?

- Do you know anyone who is an expert in a field that will help you tell your story? If so, arrange to interview them and record their answers.

- How would you describe your story to someone in just a sentence or two? (Logline)

- What are you trying to say with this story? (Theme)

- What does the voice of the piece sound like? (Tone)

- Who inhabits this world? What are their backgrounds, flaws, hopes, and dreams? What compels them to do what they do? (Characters)

- What is your basic story? (Story Summary)

- What previously published or produced works are close in genre, tone, and structure to your story? Make a list, then study and breakdown those works.

6. This Draft's for You

Things to Remember:

- Don't share your original story with anyone before you've written your first draft. Let it develop free from outside influence.

- The real reason you write is to experience the joy of expressing yourself. Never lose touch with this simple fact.

- No matter how much you've written in your life you must still start at square one each time, and make each story work in its own unique way.

- Every story you write is an exorcism, a way of freeing yourself from thoughts or feelings you can't quite resolve any other way.

- The moment you give your script to someone else to read, you have given it to the world. There is no turning back.

Questions to Ask Yourself:

- How is your life experience shaping this work? What's going on in your life right now that you're struggling with? What villainy, past or present, are you personally trying to overcome?

- How can you infuse the struggles of your personal life into your story's main conflict? How can you infuse them into your main character?

- Have you done absolutely everything with your first draft that you set out to do? Don't leave any stone unturned.

- Are you 100% sure that you're ready to give your script to someone for feedback? Are you truly ready to let it be shaped by the common culture?

7. The Art of Giving Notes

Things to Remember:

- If you understand how to give good notes to another writer, you will have a much better understanding of what to do with notes, good or bad, when you receive them.

- Have a constructive attitude when giving notes to another writer. Make them feel that you are on their team.

- Always offer concrete ideas that writers can potentially use to improve their story. Don't just identify problems.

- All writers need encouragement more than anything else, especially writers who are just starting out.

- It's always easier to see flaws in other writers' work than it is to see them in your own. Have some empathy and some humility.

- Giving good notes on a story takes work. Make sure you're committed before you agree to take the plunge.

- Focus your notes on the "big idea" of the writer's story.

- Focus your notes on the writer's setups and payoffs.

- Focus your notes on the writer's characters.

Questions to Ask Yourself:

- What is the writer trying to say? Is the message clear? If not, this is a great place to begin your note-giving process.

- What are the three most salient notes that you can give that "reverberate" with the theme of the writer's work?

- If a moment in the writer's story isn't working, is there a moment earlier in the narrative that didn't quite set it up adequately? Chances are, there is.

- Does the behavior of each character make sense for the situation?

- What does each character want in each scene?

- What does each character want from the other characters in the story?

- What does each character want on a deeper, subconscious level?

8. The Art of Receiving Notes

Things to Remember:

- Keep an open mind.

- Your story will never stop being told and is in a constant state of change.

- There is nothing precious about your story but its core message.

- Shape the notes you receive by asking follow-up questions and getting more specifics out of your note givers. *Mine for gold.*

- Always value your note givers' opinions.

- Ignore the notes you don't think are useable. Don't waste time arguing about them.

- Choose your note givers wisely, according to their strengths and taste in material.

Questions to Ask Yourself:

- Which notes apply to the core message of your story and which apply to specific details?

- Which notes support your core message? Which ones don't?

- What follow-up questions can you ask that will help shape the notes into usable ideas?

- Are any of the notes from multiple note givers the same? Chances are those notes are valid.

- Are there any notes that felt right but that your note giver couldn't quite articulate? What was their intuition trying to tell you? What was the note beneath their note?

- How invested in your success is your note giver?

9. The Art of Executing Notes

Things to Remember:

- Once you're ready to start your rewrite, it's time to tune out your note giver. *The note giver has left the building.*

- A major revision means there are significant changes that need to be made to the structure of the story.

- A minor revision may involve adding or removing selected scenes, but mostly entails revising action and dialogue within the existing structure.

- Don't be afraid to go back to the white board or the index cards to execute your rewrite.

- Be prepared to let go of every scene.

- Use a double-yellow-pad approach, writing down the current structure on one pad, and the new one on another.

- Be patient. Don't start composing the new scenes until you're absolutely confident with the new structure.

- Once you have your new structure, make a battle plan, describing within the body of your script how you are going to modify each scene.

- Consider giving your note giver the battle plan for more notes before executing the rewrite.

Questions to Ask Yourself:

- What is the scope of your rewrite? Is it a major or a minor one?

- How long do you think your rewrite is going to take? Make an estimate and see how accurate you are.

- Are there components (individual scenes or sequences) of your old structure you can use as templates for parts of your new structure?

- Is each modification you're making consistent with your core message?

10. Writing Partners

Things to Remember:

- Being in a writing partnership is like being in a marriage. It's an intimate relationship that needs to be based on trust, mutual respect, and commitment.

- The partner process takes time to evolve. You have to work at it.

- It's usually best to be in the same room with one another through the brainstorming, concept, and structuring phases.

- Once you begin outlining, it's easier to be in separate spaces, passing documents back and forth.

- Remain passionate about your ideas, but always be willing to compromise with your partner.

Questions to Ask Yourself:

- Are you willing to give up creative ownership of the work and be a 50-50 partner in it?

- Are you prepared to negotiate every creative decision with your partner if necessary?

- Are you willing to sacrifice your own voice as a writer for the sake of the voice that emerges as a product of the partnership?

- What creative ground rules have you set for your process? Under what circumstances is it okay to rewrite your partner and vice versa?

- Are you dividing the workload equally? Try not to cross the 50-yard line too often.

11. Pitching Stories

Things to Remember:

- Pitching is a necessary evil. You must be able to express your ideas verbally as well as on paper in order to give potential employers confidence that you can do the job.

- The most important thing you're selling when pitching a story is yourself. So pitch your personality.

- A pitch is a performance in which you are both the actor and the main character.

- Memorize your pitch, then perform it as though you're saying the words for the first time, just like a good actor.

- Hone your pitch so you use as few words as possible. Try to make it no longer than 10 to 15 minutes.

- When pitching with a partner, figure out ahead of time exactly who is going to say what and when.

- Be open and flexible. Anything can happen once you get in the room.

Questions to Ask Yourself:

- What's your natural storytelling style? Are you big and gregarious? Quiet and soft-spoken?

- How do you tell stories to your friends or family members in everyday life? Develop an approach that is similar.

- Is there a hook to your pitch you can use to start it off right? A personal anecdote, for example, or a metaphor that frames the theme of your story and sets the tone for the rest of the pitch?

- Which parts of your story can be edited out in your verbal presentation? Look hard at each beat as you rehearse and only include what's absolutely necessary.

- Who are you pitching to? Have you pitched to them before? Tailor your pitch to receive the most favorable response possible.

12. Writing for Hire

Things to Remember:

- You need great writing samples in order to get work for hire, which means writing on spec is essential.

- When you work as a writer for hire there is no draft for you. It's a *we* thing, not a *me* thing, from the very beginning.

- Your process is more important than ever when writing for hire. It's the one thing you can always fall back on to get you through the rocky moments.

- When you work as a writer for hire, the note giver is always right.

- As a writer, there will always be some degree of tension involved in the relationship between you and your employer. It's okay. Just accept it.

- If you're taking a writing class, approach the work as if it's a job. Don't be a writing student, be a writer for hire.

- Always have a passion project going on in the back of the shop. It will feed your soul.

Questions to Ask Yourself:

- What can you do to make the working relationship with your employer as productive as possible?

- Which are the most important battles to fight with respect to the work? Choose wisely. You can't win them all.

- How can you use your creative talent to solve any issue that arises between you and your employer, writing-related or otherwise?

- Which is better for the project (and for your career)—to be effective or to be right?

- If you're a writing student, what are the ways in which you can effectively turn your class into a work for hire? What do you want to get from your teacher? From your peers? Write down some goals.

- How can you shape the notes you get in class into something that is consistent with your vision?

13. Art vs. Commerce

Things to Remember:

- Financial success and writing success are not joined at the hip.

- You can learn the business of being a writer. But you also have to be lucky to be financially successful.

- The best way to get lucky is to be ready when luck comes your way—which means having a great script in your pocket.

- Writing success = writer gene + process. It's a marathon, not a sprint.

- Only you know when you have achieved writing success.

Questions to Ask Yourself:

• What is the definition of financial success for you as a writer? Write it down.

• Have you looked at your overall writing process and identified places where you need to improve?

• What can you do differently on your next project, process-wise, that might help you overcome some of the deficiencies in your last one?

• Have you rewritten the story you're currently working on as much as you possibly can? Do you know in your heart that it is as good as you can make it?

14. The Write Community

Things to Remember:

• To whatever extent possible, make every effort to surround yourself with a community of other writers throughout every stage of your career.

- Writers need other writers not just for moral support, but also for the exchange of energy and ideas.

- Your community of writers is your umbilical cord to numerous resources, potential collaborators, and representatives.

- Being part of a community of writers helps you express who you are as an artist.

- One of the best ways to cultivate a community of writers is to start or join a writing group.

Questions to Ask Yourself:

- Do you know any writers who are as serious about writing as you are? Who are they? Make a list.

- Have you ever sat down and had an in-depth conversation about process with these writers? How are your processes different?

- Is there anything these other writers do that you might experiment with? Anything useful that you think you might be able to incorporate into your process?

- What aspects of your process can you share with them?

- Do you know five to ten other writers who might make a good writing group? Do you know of any existing writing groups that you might be able to join?

15. Live to Write Another Day

Things to Remember:

- As creative storytellers, we are the cultural record keepers of our generation.

- Be the hero of your own story. Never give up!

- Don't be afraid to fail. No great story was ever written by a writer playing it safe.

- Your voice is worthy of being heard, and the fight to make it heard is never in vain.

AFTERWORD

Interactive Media and the Future of Storytelling

Without a doubt, the most unique aspect of my entertainment career is that in addition to working in the traditional mediums, I've also worked in so many different quarters of the interactive media business and in so many different capacities. I've been a writer on numerous projects, as well as an interactive designer, a voice director, a producer, and a creative director. My many adventures have taken me from developing PC games (back in the days of CD-ROMs), to online games, to console video games (Xbox, PlayStation etc.), to interactive theme park attractions.

The common thread that's allowed me to navigate these many worlds has been my ability to tell a story, my writer gene, coupled with the growing need these emerging art forms have for good storytellers. I want to be careful, however, not to mislead you into thinking that interactive media is a land of milk and honey for writers. The fact is, this is an industry that's very much in its infancy, one in which technology is still ahead of creativity and, at the moment, employs writers in a variety of different ways, from copywriters to pure dialogue writers to writer/designers to narrative directors. There's also no real industry-wide standard in terms of the format in which writers work. Unlike screenplays or teleplays, which pretty much all look the same, if you were to study five different interactive scripts, they would probably vary quite dramatically in how they look, how they're structured, and how they balance creative content with technical design.

For these and many other reasons, the subject of interactive writing really merits a much lengthier, in-depth discussion in its own right; however my intention here is to give you a relatively high-level treatment that focuses more on the impact interactive technology has had (and will continue to have) on us as writers, as well as on the entertainment world as a whole.

Emotions and Games

For as long as I can remember the most hotly debated topic in the gaming world has revolved around the question of whether or not you can experience genuine emotion while playing a video game. Naturally, like everyone else I have a theory about this, though mine is a very nuanced one.

Yes, I think you can experience genuine emotion while playing a video game, but it's not the same kind of emotion that you experience while consuming a traditional narrative.

Remember in Chapter 2 when I said writing involves both *passively* listening while at the same time *actively* composing? I believe a similar thing happens when you're button mashing some hideous mythological monster to death. You're passively receiving the cues that the game is constantly giving you and at the same time actively trying to beat the stuffing out of that thing. When you write, you don't typically get *emotional* about what you're doing (though I'm sure every writer has their moments). You're focused on accomplishing something. The same thing is true when you're playing a game. Even if there are some deeper emotional elements to the experience, you're only partially engaged with them because you're driven by a different kind of emotion, something I describe as an intense *need to achieve.*

On the other hand, when you watch a movie or a TV show or read a novel, you can easily become deeply emotional. That's because the experience is *entirely passive.* You're focused on receiving information, with no need to achieve anything. The dominant feeling is one of empathy for the characters you see on the screen or for whom you're reading about. This reaction is utterly visceral because storytelling is an archetypal ritual, one our ancestors have engaged in for thousands of years, predisposing us to respond in this way.

So, if the two experiences do indeed affect us in fundamentally different physiological ways, then how could we possibly expect them to elicit similar feelings or emotions? And should they? Do video games really need to be more like movies, and do all stories need to be deeply emotional in order to be good? I don't think so. You don't have to look any further than the perennial success of high-tech spy novels, like those popularized by Tom Clancy, and procedural TV crime dramas, like *CSI* and *Law & Order*, to answer that question.

Now, could I be convinced otherwise that playing a video game can be a deeply empathic and emotional experience? Given the rapid advancement of technology, and the possibilities that will undoubtedly emerge in the future, absolutely. I believe *anything* is possible.

Narrative and Interactive Design

When it comes to narrative storytelling, there's no question a prominent seat at the table exists not just for video games, but for many other types of interactive experiences as well. The challenge is that virtually all of our previous narrative formats have evolved out of the oral tradition. While a narrative *wants* to be linear and set in stone, interactive design is pretty much the opposite. It wants to be non-linear and allow the user some degree of autonomy as to how they consume the experience.

What you have in many video games is a lot of narrative delivered through backstory. In other words, you're free to explore the world the game designers have created, solve puzzles, and/or perform missions that can be completed in multiple ways. As a result, you uncover the story of events that happened in the past. I really like games that do this effectively, where the more you play, the more you learn and understand about how this particular world came to be.

Most video games also deliver narrative through the use of what are commonly called *cutscenes* or *cinematics*, which are essentially a sequence of movie scenes shoe-horned between the missions. When the game is completed, these scenes collectively tell the entire story. Personally, I have never found this method to be very satisfying because it usually takes control away from the player (i.e., stops the game) so that (A) the scenes can play at a higher resolution, and/or (B) the player is less likely to miss critical parts of the narrative. If cinematics are part of the design, I prefer them to run *in game*, which means the narrative is delivered on the fly *during* play. You may have to sacrifice a bit of the visual aesthetic, and you do risk having some story beats go unseen, but some of that can be made up for with clever design. At least this way the story feels more organic, since the active part of the experience isn't interrupted for the sake of delivering the passive part, which can be frustrating at times.

Another approach to creating interactive narrative that I have always been a big fan of involves the use of "branching" story architecture. This means multiple versions of a single over-arching story can be experienced by presenting the player with a number of different story pathways, each of which is determined, at least in part, by the choices the player makes along the way. In some cases, all paths lead to the same conclusion. In other cases, the structure provides for more than one possible outcome, which then allows players to replay the game and have a different experience.

On a practical level, creating something of this breadth is clearly an enormous amount of work. It's also an incredible writing and interactive design challenge, because not only do you have to structure and execute a single linear story (which is tough enough to do well), you also have to create a tremendous number of alternative scenes as well as somehow find a way to bring each story path to its logical and inevitable conclusion.

How About a Little More Character?

One area of narrative game design that presents a wealth of potential opportunities is the area of character. As we discussed earlier, characters and their motivations are the fundamental drivers of stories. Yet in most narrative-based games, the wants and desires of characters are often incidental to the actions that the player is required to make in order to progress through the experience. So the question that I've been asking for years is:

Why can't character motivation be more of an integral part of gameplay?

Here's an example. I'm a big World War II buff, so the early *Call of Duty* games were among my favorites, *Call of Duty 2: Big Red One* in particular. This type of game is generally called a "first-person shooter" because you see everything from the point of view of the character you're playing as you run around shooting things. In this case, you're a soldier in the thick of the European theater of battle, and there's a platoon of other GIs who accompany you throughout the entire experience. As with most games in this genre, the missions are very repetitive puzzle-solving activities in which you have to navigate a maze-like battlefield, fight your way through a horde of relentless Nazis, and ultimately complete a climactic task (like blow up a trio of anti-aircraft guns, capture a farmhouse, get to the top of a hill, etc.).

One of the many things I liked about *Big Red One* was that the NPCs (non-playing characters) in the platoon stay with you from mission to mission, shouting random commentary for the duration of the game. You also get to know a little about each one of them from brief cutscenes that take place before and after each mission, though all of this is just filler and has no impact on the actual gameplay itself.

Then, at a certain point in the middle of the game, an interesting thing happens: One of the NPC characters suddenly dies, and before you even realize what's going on, this very somber moment occurs in which a couple of the other NPCs grieve the loss of their fallen comrade. The game then quickly transitions to the next mission without skipping a beat, and there is no mention of the event again.

I'll never forget the feeling I had at that moment. Up until then I had been mindlessly blowing away all those Nazis for the pure pleasure of it, but now suddenly my writer gene had awoken and my thoughts were racing. What if we really got to know these guys in this platoon? What if instead of running around mission after mission doing variations of the same thing, the missions were about accomplishing objectives that *mattered* to your platoon mates? What if they also involved interacting with the enemy soldiers? What if you actually got to know who *those* guys were and *all* these interactions mattered? And what if there were consequences that would determine the course of the story depending on what you did and when you did it?

You see where I'm going with this? Granted, this is a shooter game, and its designers never intended for it to be about all these character-based motivations, but if you're going to introduce characters and try to tell a story, why not make that story a sincere part of the entire experience? Why not try to fuse the interactive design as much as you possibly can with the narrative?

Even if the creators of *Big Red One* only went a step or two in the direction that I'm suggesting, I'm sure they could have constructed a very interesting interactive story, making what was already a very well-designed game even better.

Being a Designer/Writer

Achieving this kind of seamless marriage of gameplay and narrative requires two things. First, there needs to be a willingness on the part of game development companies to allow the stories of their narrative-based games to be created concurrently with gameplay and level design. Typically, this isn't the case. Story details are often added much later on in the process. Second, it requires that these companies have writers working on their projects that are also skilled interactive designers. What I'm talking about now are people who not only have the writer gene, but who have the *interactive gene* as well.

You don't have to be a software engineer to be a designer/writer of interactive games, but you do have to have a fundamental understanding of how games are programmed. Obviously this is a topic that is far too complex for me to go into in great detail, but I will give you a basic introduction.

The underlying principle of all interactive design is what is commonly known as the *if/then scenario.* In other words, if *Action A* occurs, then *Result A* happens. But if *Action B* occurs, then *Result B* happens. And from there a myriad of mind-twisting possibilities ensues.

Let's say we're making my version of that character-driven WWII game. One tiny slice of what would potentially be a very extensive interactive design document for that game might go something like this:

INT. BARN – DAY OR NIGHT
IF the player enters the barn, THEN they encounter STAFF SERGEANT JOHNANNES SCHMIDT.

IF the player shoots at Schmidt, THEN Schmidt yells a battle cry and engages the player in a firefight.

IF the player kills Schmidt, THEN they will find a codebook on him. But it is written in German and they must find a way to crack the code.

IF the player gets close enough to Schmidt during the encounter and hits him with the butt of their rifle, THEN Schmidt falls to the floor unconscious and they have captured him.

IF the player captures Schmidt, THEN they will find a codebook on him. The "Interrogation Interface" now appears, allowing the player to engage in conversation with Schmidt.

By opening up a series of dialogue options, the player would then unlock various elements of the meta-plot of the story, allowing them to take further actions. This could involve cracking the code in the codebook, wiping out the remaining Germans in the town, acquiring valuable intelligence critical to the larger war effort, or perhaps even forming an unexpected bond with Sergeant Schmidt that could complicate things later with the player's platoon mates.

On the other hand, if the player kills Sergeant Schmidt, a whole other set of options and potential story paths could be opened up. Maybe there's a revenge plot that could play out involving one of Schmidt's comrades. Or maybe Schmidt's uniform becomes wearable so the player can now attempt a clandestine mission behind enemy lines that they would not have been able to engage in otherwise.

You get the idea? The possibilities are endless. This is what makes designing and writing interactive games both incredibly challenging and a lot of fun. If your brain is wired to think in terms of stories that can be told on multiple levels, like mine is, then you probably have the interactive gene as well as the writer gene—and a potential future telling these exciting new kinds of stories.

Theme Park Experiences

In recent years I have spent a great deal of time working for Walt Disney Imagineering, creating interactive experiences for Disney's theme parks and cruise ships. One of the most interesting things about WDI is that it actually started as WED, Walter Elias Disney Enterprises and, as the story goes, was the passion project in the back of Walt's shop, the shop in this case being Walt Disney Studios and the passion project, Disneyland.

Walt's vision of building the "happiest place on earth" obviously turned out pretty well, but it's the creative spirit of Imagineering that I think is his real legacy, his dedication to give artists of all different stripes, from illustrators to ride engineers to rock sculptors, the freedom to dream big and believe there's no limit to what they're capable of, which is why I have always felt right at home there.

The nice thing about working for any part of the Walt Disney Company is that you never have to look too far to find great storytelling. When you're talking about theme parks, however, you're talking about storytelling of a slightly different nature. This is *thematic* storytelling through the creative use of a wide variety of different disciplines: architecture, engineering, and advanced technologies, as well as set design, signage, sound, music, live performances, and all different kinds of interactions with walk-around characters and park operators, or as Disney prefers to call them, "cast members."

Every ride experience also tells its own unique story—a story that has been thoughtfully conceived throughout the development process and informs every aspect of the finished product. My favorite example of this is Expedition Everest, a phenomenal rollercoaster at Disney's Animal Kingdom in Orlando, Florida. The ride features a monstrous Himalayan peak that can be seen from almost anywhere in the park, and casts the legendary yeti of Asian folklore as the star of the show. Everything about the experience, from the museum-type artifacts and discarded mountain gear in the queue, to the railroad-themed ride cars, to the appearance of the abominable snow beast himself, is meticulously structured and designed to tell a satisfying story.

Ride queues in particular present interesting opportunities for storytelling. One of the many projects that I've done for WDI, Soarin'—Living Landscapes, an interactive experience located at Walt Disney World's Epcot Center (also in Orlando), presented just such an opportunity.

If you've ever had the pleasure of waiting in a long line to enjoy a ride at a theme park, I'm sure you would appreciate the work that we did with this one, because at the height of summer this particular wait could be as long as two hours. So the challenge here was to turn part of the queue, which sits in a 150-foot hallway, into an entertainment venue, thereby turning the time spent by the waiting crowd into something fun and memorable.

After a fairly extensive technology exploration, we decided the most effective approach would be to use "computer vision," which is the same technology now used in the Microsoft Kinect video-game console. Using cameras to sense the body movements of our guests, we would then be able to create a series of short, three- to five-minute, graphical video-game-type experiences (projected onto movie-theater-sized screens) that they could engage in using only their bodies as an interface. The difference between our project and what Kinect would do some three years later is that we would use *five* cameras, each of which would capture up to *fifty* people, while the Kinect would use only one camera and would be able to look at only one person at a time. Our goal was to create a mass audience gaming system in which up to *two hundred fifty* people could participate at once!

As the creative director, writer, and producer of the project, I led a team of engineers, artists, and interactive designers through a series of brainstorming sessions. Over a number of months I would continually write and rewrite draft outlines detailing the proposed guest interaction of the five experiences that we would eventually produce and install at Epcot. Our most ambitious effort, called Balloon Odyssey, is perhaps the best example of how we were able to tell an interactive story using this very unique venue.

When the game begins, a hot air balloon sits atop a beautiful vista next to a shining castle, adorned with sparkling jewels. All is well in paradise. The kingdom is peaceful and serene. But then suddenly, ominous music rises, as a "bandit balloon" enters the frame, steals the jewels by sucking them up with a giant vacuum, and makes off with the loot (Act One). Following this, the "hero balloon" is launched, sailing after the bandit in hot pursuit. It's now up to the fifty guests standing in front of each screen to steer their hero balloon through a series of obstacles (by controlling it with their collective body movements) in order to recover the stolen treasure (Act Two). Mythological creatures, craggy rock formations, and fierce weather threaten the hero balloon every step of the way, until the guests eventually bring it in for a safe landing back at the castle, after which each team receives a final score based on how many jewels they were able to recover (Act Three).

I'll be the first to admit that Balloon Odyssey is a pretty unusual narrative driven in a most unusual way, but like all the games in the Living Landscapes installation, it's a remarkably satisfying experience, one that I'm proud to say has run every single day, 365 days a year, since it was installed on July 4, 2007.

Transmedia Storytelling

Before the proliferation of the Internet in the mid-1990s, entertainment properties pretty much stayed in their own neat little boxes. The only consistent crossover we saw were plays, novels, and other written materials turned into movies, and movies eventually migrating to television. But for well over a decade now, we've seen an explosion of two-way migration between all sorts of original properties, from comic books and graphic novels, to video games, to movies, to television, to the web. We've seen interactive marketing campaigns of all different types, using all different technologies, pitching all different kinds of products. And we've seen the emergence of casual online and mobile games that are not only available on both platforms, but are able to be viewed and played on each, within the course of the experience (for example, you can make a move in *Words With Friends*, either on your phone or on your computer through Facebook, and the game tracks your progress on both devices).

All this cross-pollination of creative content has also given birth to a new form of narrative called *transmedia storytelling* in which a fictional universe is created that allows for a story to be told across multiple mediums simultaneously.

What's exciting about the transmedia movement is that stories are now being developed that are intended to be delivered across different mediums from the initial conception of the idea, not just as a way to take advantage of a secondary market. When you add to that the speed of technology advancement and the openness of younger generations to consume entertainment in new and different ways, it's not hard to imagine a world in which these kinds of platforms could become extremely popular.

Recently a very forward-thinking company hired me to write an animated television pilot that would also lay the foundation for what I thought was a very smart transmedia strategy. The challenge was to write the pilot in the traditional way, using a four-act structure that allows the resulting twenty-two-minute episode to have multiple commercial breaks while having each act be somewhat self-contained so that it could potentially be viewed online as a five-minute webisode. In addition, each script had to contain at least one *set piece* that could serve as the framework for a casual online game. In other words, we had to create a story that could stand on its own, be broken into four stand-alone parts, *and* have at least one scene with a clearly exploitable gaming element. There would also be a social networking component built into the website, merchandising, sponsorship opportunities, and the potential to create a full-length feature film based on the property.

This strategy not only gave the producers the option of delivering the linear content either online or on television, it also carved out space for original stories to be delivered via interactive games, opening up the possibility of allowing the larger narrative to unfold and expand simultaneously across the mediums.

This new paradigm is one of the most exciting developments in entertainment to come along in many years, especially for writers with the interactive gene. Only time will tell how this kind of narrative will be received, and what formats will eventually take hold and break into the popular culture, but make no mistake, transmedia storytelling is coming soon to a cell phone, iPad, and computer near you!

Story as a Living Three-Dimensional Experience

Finally, I think it's only appropriate to conclude our little adventure by sharing with you my own vision of a future storytelling medium that I think has very exciting potential. I like to call it:

Story as a Living Three-Dimensional Experience.

Using the advanced processing power we will begin to see in all the new devices in the next few years (computers, smartphones, tablets, and computerized televisions), I see us being able to create photorealistic worlds that can be navigated in much the same way you navigate a video game. But this isn't a game I'm talking about. It's a story you essentially *step into* and experience voyeuristically.

Imagine a live HD video feed that allows you to move through space as if you *are* the camera. You have the ability to go anywhere within this world—walk down the street, go to the park, go into retail stores, enter private offices, apartments, bedrooms, basements…anywhere. As you do, you encounter various characters playing out various scenes. You then have the ability to follow these characters and watch their stories unfold. In fact, you have the ability to experience every character and every location the world provides. When you return to certain locations at a later time, you see new beats of the story that you hadn't seen before. All these beats build on one another, forming an interconnected narrative that is revealed scene by scene based on what you have previously experienced—a narrative that starts to make more and more sense the more you explore and the more time you spend in the world.

Instead of being a passive linear experience that you sit back and watch, you actively seek the story out and watch it unfold all around you by essentially living *inside* it. It's an active, non-linear experience in which you choose to receive the various facets of the story in the order you want.

Creating such an experience would be similar to writing a television show with a large ensemble cast, where many storylines exist in parallel and intersect at various points along the overall arc of the larger narrative. And like television, these stories can continue in perpetuity, for as long as you (the creator) want them to. The difference is, once you launch this new type of "show," you would not be restricted to writing episodes in self-contained thirty- or sixty-minute units. Instead, you would simply begin to add more scenes to whichever storylines you wish, whenever you wish, creating a living three-dimensional experience that continues to expand and grow in different directions.

The technological framework on which this system would be built would also allow you to track the parts of your world where your audience is spending the most time, as well as enable you to communicate with them directly. In this way, you and your writing staff could concentrate and expand upon the storylines where you're getting the most enthusiastic response.

This is the kind of revolutionary storytelling that interactive technology gives us. Now it's up to us, as writers, to take advantage of this monumental opportunity and create the defining entertainment mediums of the future.

ABOUT THE AUTHOR

Fresh out of the wonderful academic cocoon of Bates College in 1986, Dean Orion began his career as a professional writer by crafting copy for a local ad agency in his native Long Island by day and hopping trains to The Lee Strasberg Creative Center in New York City, where his first play, *Weekend In My Mind*, was produced by night.

After moving to Los Angeles in 1988 to attend The American Film Institute, briefly working for CBS Productions, and successfully mounting another of his plays, *A Comedy Of Eros* at the Beverly Hills Playhouse, Dean soon discovered that the long and very eclectic winding road of his career was only just beginning.

With the sale of *Maelstrom* in 1995, an original graphical adventure game purchased by special effects company Digital Domain, Dean suddenly found himself telling stories in remarkably new ways. Since then he has written, designed, produced, and directed an extensive and wide array of interactive content for CD-ROM, DVD, online, and console games.

Dean's interactive credits include such console titles as *Van Helsing* and *Mission Impossible: Operation Surma*; massively multiplayer online games, *Guild Wars* and *Aion;* Nintendo DS and Wii titles *iCarly* and *The Penguins Of Madagascar;* as well as numerous casual online games for Hollywood marketing campaigns, including such notable tent poles as *The X-Files, Men In Black, Terminator 2: Judgment Day, Mission To Mars,* and *Independence Day,* just to name a few.

Managing this split personality between writing traditional linear and non-linear interactive content has never been easy, but Dean has always found a way to do both, writing freelance episodes of such television shows as *The Invisible Man* for Syfy, *Thought Crimes* for USA Network, and *Jackie Chan Adventures* for WB Kids. Recently, Dean wrote the American pilot for the internationally acclaimed animated television series *Ben and Izzy* for Rubicon Studios, and penned *Newburgh* and *I Am An American Soldier,* two short films for The National Museum of The United States Army.

Dean's unique background has also led him into the world of themed entertainment, where he has worked for many years as a writer, show producer, and creative director for Walt Disney Imagineering. Among the high-profile projects that he has helped create for WDI are *Virtual Jungle Cruise,* which opened at the DisneyQuest arcade in Orlando, Florida, in 1998; *Soarin'– Living Landscapes,* a large-scale interactive gaming system that opened at Epcot Center in 2007; and *The Magic Playfloor*, an interactive floor installed on Disney Cruise Line's new Dream and Fantasy cruise ships, which launched in 2011 and 2012, respectively.

A member of the Writers Guild of America, Dean has sat on the guild's New Media Caucus steering committee and has been a featured speaker at several guild-sponsored events, including panels for the 2006 Game Developers Conference in San Jose, California, and the Writers Guild Foundation in 2008.

To contact Dean and learn more about The Writer Gene online community for writers please visit www.thewritergene.com.